Lt.Col. A. J. N. BARTLETT, D.S.O. (and bar)
Commanded June 1916 to March 1919.

War Record
of the
1/4th Battalion
Oxfordshire & Buckinghamshire
Light Infantry.

Compiled by
MAJOR P. PICKFORD, D.S.O., M.C.

The Naval & Military Press Ltd

Published by
The Naval & Military Press Ltd
5 Riverside, Brambleside, Bellbrook
Industrial Estate, Uckfield, East Sussex,
TN22 1QQ England

Tel: +44 (0) 1825 749494
Fax: +44 (0) 1825 765701

www.naval-military-press.com
www.nmarchive.com

In reprinting in facsimile from the original, any imperfections are inevitably reproduced and the quality may fall short of modern type and cartographic standards.

Dedicated by permission

to

MAJOR-GENERAL SIR R. FANSHAWE,
K.C.B., D.S.O.,

Late Oxfordshire and Buckinghamshire
Light Infantry,

Who commanded the 48th (South Midland) Division
from June 1915 to June 1918.

ERRATA.

PAGE 13, line 12—For "enemy" read "existing."

PAGE 49, last line—For "SEMILIE" read S. EMILIE.

PAGE 50, line 19—After "G.O.C.-in-C's" insert "Despatch."

PAGE 67, line 22—For "Hutchins" read "Hutchings."

PAGE 68, line 30—For "Shayler" read "Shaylor."

PAGE 83, line 4—For "200005 Cpl. C. E. Lieberman" read "200015 Cpl. W. L. Lieberman."

TABLE OF CONTENTS.

FRONTISPIECE - - - LT.-COL. A. J. N. BARTLETT

	PAGE
DIARY OF THE WAR	1
EXTRACTS FROM OFFICIAL DESPATCHES	49
CASUALTIES	53
KILLED IN ACTION	54
HONOURS AND AWARDS	73
OFFICIAL RECORD OF AWARDS	85
OFFICERS MARCH 1915 AND DECEMBER 1918	105
OFFICERS HOLDING VARIOUS APPOINTMENTS	109
ROLL OF OFFICERS	111
ROLL OF WARRANT OFFICERS AND SERGEANTS	119
ROLL OF SERGEANTS OVERSEAS	121
ROLL OF N.C.O'S. AND MEN WHO SERVED THROUGHOUT THE CAMPAIGN	125

MAPS.

SKETCH MAP OF POZIERES BATTLEFIELD	17
SKETCH MAP OF PERONNE AREA	27

DIARY OF THE WAR.

ENGLAND.
August 1914
to
March 1915.

1914.

On August 2nd, war was imminent when the Battalion Aug. 2
went into camp at MARLOW for its annual training,
only to be re-called to OXFORD within 24 hours, on the Aug. 3
day before war was actually declared. The next few days Aug. 4
were fully occupied in enrolling recruits, who were posted
to companies delightfully quartered and fêted in different
colleges. Our colours were deposited in the Cathedral, Aug. 6
and a few days later we were sent to SWINDON, where Aug. 9
the SOUTH MIDLAND Division was concentrated.

Here we were fitted up with transport and stores and
remained a week. We then went by train to LEIGHTON Aug. 16
BUZZARD, and marched eight miles to DUNSTABLE.
After some days spent here, the invasion scare arose,
and we were marched on successive days to HITCHIN, Aug. 20
to WARE, to SAWBRIDGEWORTH, to DUNMOW, to GREAT
WALTHAM, eventually arriving at WRITTLE, near Chelms- Aug. 25
ford. We were expecting to move on the next day to the
coast, but stayed seven months, and were treated royally
by the inhabitants, who very philosophically accepted the
added fifty per cent. to their population.

At Writtle we were made up to War Establishment,
and settled down to strenuous but congenial training,
varied by occasional outings to Dunstable, to Colchester,
or to Purfleet for range practice, and, later, by a less
welcome day's shooting at Boreham, which involved a

A

2 WAR RECORD OF THE

Sept. 2 long and tedious march. In September the Division, which was concentrated round Chelmsford, marched
Oct 14 past General Sir IAN HAMILTON in the course of a 24 mile route march, and in October the Division was
1915. reviewed by the KING in HYLANDS PARK.
Jan. 30 In January the four company organisation was adopted and Company Commanders were mounted for the first time; many amusing episodes relating to horses and senior officers belong to this period.

Always haunted by the fear of not getting to France before the war was over, and incredibly jealous of the London Scottish and other more favoured Territorial Battalions, we at length, in March, 1915, began to make active preparation to go overseas. When we eventually
Mar. 29 marched out of WRITTLE the entire population was assembled round the Green to see us off and wish us well, and we left behind a very discontented surplus of 100 men, mostly under nineteen, who were to join us a few months later.

"PLUG STREET."
April 1915
to
June 1915.

Leaving CHELMSFORD in two trains at 7 p.m., we embarked at FOLKESTONE at 11.30 p.m. on the S.S.
Mar. 30 ONWARD and disembarked at BOULOGNE about 1 a.m., where we marched to the Rest Camp, greeted in the streets of the town by many curious glances from window shutters half thrown back, as the inhabitants were wakened by the tramp of nailed boots on the cobble

stones. The Rest Camp was situated in tents on a bleak hill, and we spent the coldest night within memory: the icy shave in the morning will not soon be forgotten by those who experienced it.

At 2 p.m. we entrained at the little station of PONT DE BRIQUES, and were conveyed by way of CALAIS and S. OMER to CASSEL—our first experience of the now familiar trucks labelled "*Hommes* 40 *Chevaux* 8." We arrived about 8 p.m., and, after an interminable wait while the transport was unloaded, marched about seven miles to farm billets near STEENWOORDE, which we did not reach until midnight to find that the local guides had gone to bed; it was long before we all got settled down on the straw, and from lack of experience in billeting some of us spent a bad night sleeping in the frost. Mar. 30

At STEENWORDE the Brigade was inspected by General Sir H. SMITH-DORRIEN, and it was here that we heard guns for the first time. Apr. 2

We next marched eight miles to farms in the neighbourhood of FLETRE, and after three days we went on through BAILLEUL to OOSTHOVE FARM, near NIEPPE, where we were very closely billetted. Companies were then sent on succeeding days into the line south of PLOEGSTEERT WOOD for instruction, and we had our first experience of real trenches, of bullets arriving, of shells (we thought we had a very narrow shave when a few fell 500 yards from our farm), and of VEREY lights. The East Lancs. and the L.R.B. were very considerate to us, and were more than pleased to be relieved by our Division a few days later. Apr. 4 Apr. 7

After five days of fatigues in the wood and instruction in the line we marched back to barns between STEEN- Apr. 12

WERKE and BAILLEUL for three days, during which two officers and two sergeants went for first instruction in
Apr. 15 bombing; we then marched back to billets at PONT DE NIEPPE and ARMENTIERES, the transport going to ROMARIN, where they remained while we were in this part of the country.

Apr. 17 Our first sector of line was at PROWSE POINT, north of PLOEGSTEERT WOOD, two companies and headquarters being back at the "Piggeries," and the remainder marching up by way of HYDE PARK CORNER and relieving the 7th Argyll and Sutherland Highlanders in trenches in
Apr. 19 front of S. IVES, facing MESSINES. Two days later the Berks relieved us, and two companies went to log huts at HUNTERSTON in the wood, and two to PLOEGSTEERT village, carrying out various "fatigues" in the wood by day.

Apr. 23 Four days later we again went up to PROWSE POINT SECTOR, and held the line for four days. During this period Major R. L. OVEY took over command from Lt.-Col. F. W. SCHOFIELD.

Apr. 27 On relief (again by the Berks), we marched back to ROMARIN, but in the middle of the night we received orders to take over the BIRDCAGE SECTOR in front of
Apr. 28 PLOEGSTEERT WOOD the next day, and had to send on parties at once to take over the line. Hurried baths at PONT DE NIEPPE, followed by an extremely hot march, left us very tired on reaching the front line next afternoon. Headquarters were established at RIFLE HOUSE; two companies were in the line, another at HUNTERSTON SOUTH, and one in PLOEGSTEERT.

In this sector we stayed for 40 days and 40 nights, with inter-company reliefs every four days. On the 30th

1/4th OXF. & BUCKS LT. INFTY.   5

and on May 1st the wood, especially in the neighbour- May 1
hood of Battalion Headquarters was shelled fairly heavily:
the gas attack at Ypres had been launched, and on May
2nd we were issued with cotton-waste pads and goggles
as anti-gas measures, and orders were issued that no
officer would go to sleep. A Boche attack was expected
and at night the companies in support had to man the
breastworks which constituted the second line. Every
few days were marked by the issue of a new type of res-
pirator and by May 6th every man was in possession of
one, all troops in the front line wearing them on the
forehead when asleep.

On May 9th the British attack at FESTUBERT took May 9
place, and we had orders to carry out a series of demonstrations from our trenches. Rifles were fired over the
top at intervals, rifle grenades fired volleys into the
enemy front line, the Gamage catapult attempted to fire
bombs from the mine to the "BIRDCAGE," the mountain
guns were brought up and fired from the front line :
altogether the Boche must have been greatly entertained.

Here Lt..Col. W. F. B. R. DUGMORE, D.S.O., took over May 11
command of the Battalion.

During this long period we became very proficient in
the art of trench warfare. We were expert builders of
sand-bagged breastworks and constructed the first continuous line in front of S. IVES, while the enemy was
employed on a similar task a hundred yards or so away,
neither party attempting to molest the other. We
learned to make *chevaux de frise*, (or knife rests), which
we carried up to the front line at night, threw over the
parapet and wired together in position, as the lines were
too close together to make ordinary wiring a pleasant

6 WAR RECORD OF THE

pastime. We put steel loopholes in the parapet, and tried to compete with the excellence of the enemy sniping.

We dug a second system of trenches on HILL 63 overlooking MESSINES (which was the scene of much fighting in 1918), working by stealth on the darkest nights that have ever been, and then tramping back to our huts in the wood over the uneven " corduroy " track (as we then called it), the first such path constructed, simply formed by nailing bits of bough across two felled trees about eighteen inches apart; very convenient by day, but intolerably painful on a black night.

From " PLUG STREET " WOOD we occasionally marched to the old Brewery at PONT DE NIEPPE, which the enterprise of the 4th Division had converted into baths. Who has forgotten the huge vats (in which it was even possible to swim), and the old attendant's cry of " Any more for any more ? " ?

May 18 Other incidents of happy days at PLUG STREET were the occasion when our ration dump, ESSEX FARM, took fire, and battalion headquarters all assembled to put it out until dispersed by quite heavy shelling.

May 23 In PLUG STREET WOOD we had our first experience of " wind up." The enemy simulated an attack by shouting and showing dummies on his parapet at night in front of a battalion north of us: they opened rapid fire, the enemy did the same, and in a few seconds both sides were firing rapid on a front which must have extended for many miles, perhaps from the Swiss Frontier to the sea! Needless to add, nothing happened, and after the lapse of a quarter of an hour and the expenditure of a very

1/4th OXF. & BUCKS LT. INFTY. 7

large amount of S.A.A., everything was quiet again, and we continued to put out knife rests.

In these trenches we first had the pleasure of instructing in trench work some of the new "Kitchener Army"—The 9th SCOTTISH RIFLES in the BIRDCAGE SECTOR (May 31st), to be followed during the next year by many other battalions—the 5th R. BERKS in the DOUVE SECTOR (June 14th), the 11th R. WARWICKS (September 2nd), the 8th SHROPSHIRE L.I. (September 18th), the 10th R. IRISH RIFLES (October 11th), the 10th R. INNISKILLING FUSILIERS (October 27th), the 13th R. IRISH RIFLES (November 13th), the 20th MANCHESTERS (November 28th), and the 18th KING'S LIVERPOOLS (December 18th); all in G Sector HEBUTERNE; the 18th W. YORKS (March 22nd, 1916), and the 13th YORKS AND LANCS (March 27th, 1916); in K Sector HEBUTERNE.

Then there was the firing of the mine under the BIRDCAGE; this was one of our earliest mines, which, by dint of most strenuous labour and dogged perseverance against innumerable difficulties of soil and water, had been pushed right under the German front line. The Germans June 5 were then reported to have started a counter-mine which was rapidly nearing our shaft, and so after we had carried up five tons of gunpowder from ESSEX FARM, and marched men up and down the corduroy track as if we intended to attack, the sappers fired the mine, destroying June 6 the enemy's network of trenches at the BIRDCAGE and blowing in his mine shaft.

On the following day we were relieved and marched June 7 out to PONT DE NIEPPE where we were reviewed by Major-General R. FANSHAWE, C.B., D.S.O., on his taking June 10 over the Division from Major-General H. N. C. HEATH,

8 WAR RECORD OF THE

C.B., who left us on account of ill-health and died shortly afterwards.

June 11 On the 11th we went to the Sector below the MESSINES Hill on the RIVER DOUVE for a short "tour,"
June 15 then going back to WHITE GATES in the neighbourhood
June 19 of HYDE PARK CORNER. After a few days in hutments
June 24 in reserve near NEUVE EGLISE we began a march southwards, as it was intended that we should be used in the coming battle for LENS.

We had three long night marches, staging at VIEUX BERQUIN [25th] and GONNEHEM [26th], to ALLOUAGNE,
June 27 where we had a very pleasant stay of a fortnight, and
July 8 lined the road while Lord KITCHENER (accompanied by General FRENCH and the PRINCE OF WALES), drove past on his last tour of inspection. Bombing was then beginning to be taken seriously and the MILLS bomb was first used in practice: a serious accident unfortunately occurred, which caused the battalion ten casualties.

July 12 From ALLOUAGNE we went up to the mining district, and were bivouacked at NOEUX LES MINES in perhaps the dirtiest billets behind the line we have ever struck. Officers reconnoitred the line at VERMELLES, and we worked on support-line digging; but plans were changed,
July 17 and after a very long and wet night march to AMES we entrained at BERGUETTE for DOULLENS, marching on arrival to TERRAMESNIL, where we billeted at about 1 a.m.
July 19 From there we marched to COIGNEUX and camped in a field near the kite balloon from which BASIL HALLAM was afterwards killed.

> HEBUTERNE
> July 1915
> to
> July 1916.

Next day the officers went up to HEBUTERNE in a July 20
G.S. wagon to reconnoitre the line held by a French
Territorial* Division. We found a very quiet, peaceful
sector, consisting of miles of very deep unrevetted trenches
usually cut through the red mud, but often chiselled
right through rocky ground, with communication trenches
running back for a mile or more. In front of the front
line were saps running out into the wire, and the enemy
was 300 to 1,000 yards away.

HEBUTERNE itself had been badly battered in the heavy
fighting of October, 1915, when the French drove out
the Prussian Guards : but many houses were still fairly
intact and at first all our headquarters, and our support
billets, were in houses and barns in the village.

The French relied largely on their 75's in case of
attack, and by day had very few sentries on duty.

The same day we took the line over after much frater-
nising—all four companies up, finding their own supports,
and holding a much longer line than we were accustomed July 20
to. We began patrolling almost at once, and soon
established a principle from which we have never gone
back, viz., that No Man's Land must be our playground, July 21
and that the enemy must be kept within his own wire.

Our early days at HEBUTERNE passed without much
incident. The weather was good and we were relieved

---

* *i.e.* of men over 35.

10 WAR RECORD OF THE

July 24 by the Berks, going back after four days to billets in HEBUTERNE, and after another eight days -with three
Aug. 5 companies in the line—to SAILLY-AU-BOIS. Here we spent a week in billets which were not too comfortable, and occasionally we were shelled by a long-range gun.
Aug. 21 We then went back to HEBUTERNE and were soon afterwards transferred to G Sector—the low-lying piece
Aug. 31 of ground, dominated by SERRE, over which the French had attacked in June in an unsuccessful attempt to capture the SERRE Hill. Between this sector and the pleasant little village of COURCELLES we spent the next five months, relieving and being relieved regularly every twelve days by the 7th Worcesters, with whom we carried out a friendly rivalry with regard to work in the line and improvements in our rest billets. COURCELLES was soon transformed by the labours of the pioneers into a model village, with a concert hall, football grounds, and every luxury that was possible two miles behind the line. Barns were improved and officers' quarters made comfortable, the band of the 5th Sussex Regiment was occasionally brought over, and subsequently our own Divisional Band was formed and first played to us on December 13th, so that we soon began to regard our return to COURCELLES as going home. On one of our route marches from COURCELLES we were inspected by the Army Commander, Sir CHARLES MUNRO.

Sept. 16 Rumours of projected attacks, wire cutting, and other activity somewhat disturbed our peace of mind in the line in late September, but the LOOS attack did not succeed, and it was decided to make the best of existing conditions until the spring. Our happiness in rest billets was broken by constant and large working parties (the name "fatigues" was then barred), on an elaborate "Corps Line" behind COURCELLES.

In mid-October we had several misty mornings, which we found very useful in the front line for daylight wiring, exploration, and souvenir hunting. About this time, too, the enemy began to try to upset our nerves with a large minenwerfer, which threw over oil-drums filled with high explosive, calculated to frighten one considerably, but incapable of doing much damage, other than purely local. Our reply was the WEST Spring Gun, which threw back cricket-ball bombs into his front line, but lacked range, and was soon spotted.

On October 18th we had our first heavy shelling, when Oct. 18 the enemy, half-an-hour before a projected demonstration by our artillery, fired countless 5·9" shells into G sector and reduced many of the trenches to pulp. This was the first sign that he had brought more guns into the Sector and our first experience of the comparatively new 5·9" How. shell.

On October 25th the Battalion was chosen to repre- Oct. 25 sent the Division at a ceremonial parade at ACHEUX, on the occasion of a review by the KING and· President POINCARE.

On next going into the line the weather broke up, and Oct. 27 conditions in the unrevetted trenches dug in soft earth became very bad—trenches fell in everywhere, and incessant labour was necessary to keep any of them open at all ; men stuck in the soft mud and literally had to be dug out. By December we had abandoned communication trenches, and laid brushwood tracks overland to be used at night.

12 WAR RECORD OF THE

Dec. 31 On December 31st it occurred to both sides to celebrate the New Year with an artillery programme, but as German time was an hour in advance of ours the enemy had his little joke first : our demonstration included rockets and flares, and was more artistic.

1916. In January, enemy activity with rifle grenades and trench mortars was becoming a nuisance, and the only counter-irritant was our guns, which, however, took up the matter and put a stop to it.

Jan. 21 On the 21st we were moved to K Sector facing GOMMECOURT WOOD, and after one further spell of six days at COURCELLES, which proved to be our last, we remained continuously in the line for seven weeks. Trenches here were better in every respect, they looked down on the Boche position, and being high were for the most part dry ; communications were much shorter and consequently had been revetted and bricked. During their period in this Sector the 6th Gloucesters, on November 25th, 1915, carried out their famous raid on Gommecourt Park, and the Boche was not slow to imitate them on several occasions. Artillery activity increased very greatly, and HEBUTERNE in February became a very unhealthy place to live in. Much work was done on making substantial sandbagged structures inside houses, and we began to clear out cellars for habitation.

Steel helmets were gradually introduced, and on February 23rd a man's life was undoubtedly saved by one, after which we began to appreciate their value and to live down their discomfort. The K Sector period was not very eventful ; gas alarms in January, raid alarms in February, attack alarms in March, served to vary the monotony : even in this comparatively good sector much

1/4th OXF. & BUCKS LT. INFTY. 13

work was entailed after snow, frost and subsequent thaws.

Patrolling was, as always, an important factor, and many attempts to intercept enemy patrols near the "Z" hedge failed because of the non-appearance of the enemy. On one night every single man of one of the companies patrolled with his platoon to the famous hedge.

Not until March 21st did we even get one company back Mar. 21 from the line to BAYENCOURT, and it was April 8th— after nine weeks—before we were relieved, and the Apr. 8 Battalion got back to BAYENCOURT, only to have to return at night to dig and wire a new trench 400 yards in front of the enemy front line.

At BAYENCOURT we did our best to enjoy ourselves for eight days, and it was here that we first heard the Divisional Concert Party—the CURIOS—a somewhat belated, but none the less appreciated emulation of the 4th Division FOLLIES, whom some of us had seen nearly a year before at ARMENTIERES and again in the autumn of 1915 at ACHEUX. In this period the Battalion Scouts were started, who were later, and especially in Italy, to do such excellent work.

In May we returned to G Sector, relieving our old May 2 friends the 7th Worcesters on a greatly extended front, and had a period of six days, during which we were heavily shelled and trench-mortared and sustained many casualties. On relief we went back to huts in COUIN, and had ten days of hard work—cable-laying in the forward area in preparation for the coming offensive. The Berks who relieved us were raided and had a good many casualties from the shelling.

We then had a trying march—reviewed by the Corps May 18 Commander, Lt.-General HUNTER-WESTON, en route—

14 WAR RECORD OF THE

to BEAUVAL where we spent a fortnight in good billets: the inhabitants were very good to us, and made us very much at home. Short rifles and steel helmets were issued to everybody, and we saw with interest several demonstrations of Stokes mortars, the new arm which was to break down the enemy resistance in his front line. Peaceful company training went on, and companies marched to HEM and bathed in the AUTHIE river.

May 31 From BEAUVAL we marched back to ONEUX (six miles from ABBEVILLE) to complete our training. The village was not pleasant, the inhabitants were inclined to be hostile, and four days later we changed our quarters to

June 4 AGENVILLERS, which was a slight improvement, despite crowded billets. Here we carried out Battalion and Brigade training, and held a Brigade Horse Show, and here Lt.-Col. A. J. N. BARTLETT joined us. On June

June 10 10th we moved back to the line in two long marches with mid-day halts, staying at MEZEROLLES [10th], and COUIN [11th], (in bivouacs). The third day saw us back in G Sector, where we spent four days being shelled and trying to cope with the mud and to re-wire the Sector devastated in the raid on the BERKS.

June 16 Our next move was back to bivouacs in the "DELL," close behind SAILLY AU BOIS. The weather improved and we found large nightly parties for the line. Preparations for the great offensive were evident on all sides, guns and dumps were everywhere, registration by the heavy guns evidently made the enemy suspicious, and several aircraft came over our lines, a hitherto almost unknown impertinance.

June 22 We next went back to bivouacs between COUIN and
June 27 COIGNEUX, and while there ran some successful sports.

From here a party of 50 of the battalion attempted a raid June 29
north of THE POINT which was frustrated by masses of
still uncut wire.

We then marched to bivouacs near MAILLY-MAILLET July 1
as the great SOMME offensive started. Our camp was
pitched about 400 yards from a 15″ How. which made
rest impossible by firing every half hour day and night.

On the following day our brigade, less the Bucks July 2
battalion, was taken from reserve and ordered to push
home an attack in the early morning, our task being to
capture three lines of the enemy front system on which
yesterday's attempt had failed. We marched off at 7 p.m.,
and got into position at MESNIL by 11.30 p.m., when
orders were cancelled about three hours before zero, and
we were sent back to MAILLY-MAILLET, the attack being
abandoned north of the ANCRE. On the 3rd we reached July 3
bivouacs near COUIN and then returned once more July 4
to G Sector, to find the trenches incredibly bad, conditions
very lively, and the weather appalling. To make the
enemy even more apprehensive, if possible, we had to
"loose off" smoke on two occasions during our four
days' tour. On relief we went back into bivouacs behind July 8
SAILLY, and nightly found large parties for carrying wire,
gas cylinders, &c. On the 10th we sent up 600 men July 10
with orders to advance our front line 500 yards in front
of H Sector between the PUISIEUX and SERRE roads.
This work, which involved digging a traversed fire-trench
(with communication trenches), within 200 yards of the
enemy, was carried out extremely well in under two hours;
and in view of the extreme nervousness of the enemy the
toll of three killed and six wounded was less than might
have been expected.

16   WAR RECORD OF THE

July 12　　We then went up for our last four days in G Sector, one company (changed midway) remaining back in the DELL. A C Company patrol was heavily engaged, and another smoke demonstration evoked a terrific artillery reply from the enemy, who was hourly expecting a renewal of our unsuccessful attack of the 1st.

July 16　　On the 16th we were not sorry to see the last of G Sector, and, on relief by the 10th Welch Regiment, we went back to bivouacs between COUIN and S. LEGER, to be joined the following day by A Company, who had been left behind to help the Welsh.

SOMME.
July and
August 1916

July 17　　Then began our first experience of a real attack. We were hustled down to BOUZINCOURT in 36 motor lorries, to find ourselves in reserve in huts and orchards west of the village, (the transport being at SENLIS), and were told that the 143rd and 144th Brigades were holding OVILLERS and a front line just below POZIERES.

July 18　　On the following day we received sudden orders at 7.15 p.m. to carry out an attack at 1.30 a.m., and before any opportunity had been given for reconnaissance we were recalled from the village and marched away at once to ALBERT. Just beyond the town we drew stacks of stores for consolidating, &c., and it was zero hour as we got into position. The attack was made by C Company on the right and B on the left, with A in support and D in reserve. Owing to darkness and imperfect knowledge of the ground, the attack lost direction and

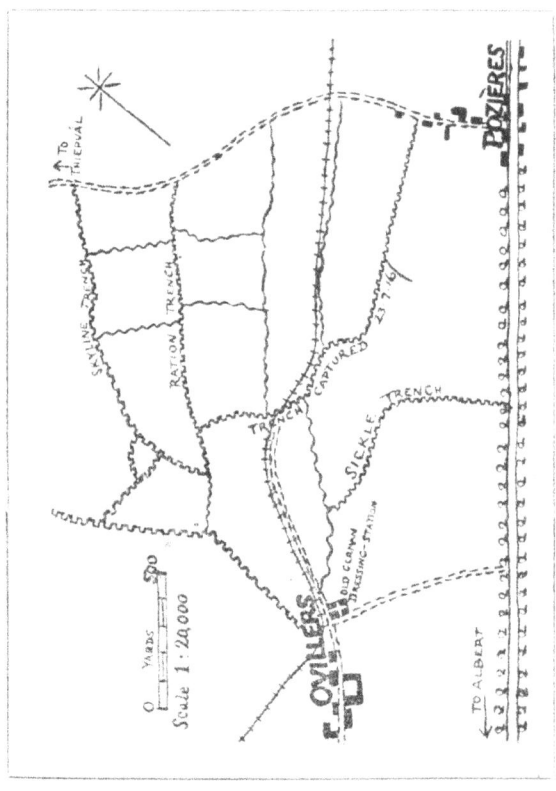

18   WAR RECORD OF THE

was broken up by machine-gun and shell fire : the battalion was then ordered to withdraw to BOUZINCOURT, having lost 20 other ranks killed, and 100 wounded, besides two officers.

July 21   Two days later we again returned at midnight and bivouacked in old gun emplacements forward of ALBERT, in reserve to a second unsuccessful attack by our brigade,
July 22   and were employed on working parties. Next day our orders were to make the same attack at 12.30 a.m. on the 23rd, subsequently to the attack on POZIERES by the Australian Division at 10 p.m. The order of battle was D on the right and A on the left, B in support to D, C in reserve ; and owing to better knowledge of the ground, all objectives were gained in spite of the most determined
July 23   enemy resistance, and several counter attacks were driven off.

Our casualties were heavy, as the enemy expected the attack and put down an intense barrage, and the shelling during the whole of the day following was very severe. At night we were relieved by the 5th Warwicks and went back by way of ALBERT to BOUZINCOURT, and after
July 24   staying there for a day and reorganising the N.C.O.'s, we
July 26   marched back to ARQUEVES, where we stayed another
July 28   day ; then to our old billets at BEAUVAL, where we were
July 29   warmly received ; and finally to AGENVILLE.

Our billets here provided a most welcome change from recent experiences. The inhabitants proved very pleasant, the orchards and lanes looked their very best, the weather was glorious, there was nothing to remind us of the ugly war three days march away. We bathed, played cricket, lay about in the orchards ; training was light, and altogether our eleven days here is, perhaps, the most delightful memory of four-and-a-half years of war. Our first drafts of "Derby men" from Devon reached us, and most of us were inoculated.

We stayed at our same billets at BEAUVAL, (which we began to regard as our second home in France), on our way back to the SOMME, the next day's march taking us to VARENNES, where billets were crowded and dirty. A third march landed us in a cornfield near BOUZINCOURT again, where we bivouacked, in preference to billeting in the village, which was being shelled a good deal.

Aug. 9

Aug. 10
Aug. 11

After a pause of one day we returned to the sordid neighbourhood of OVILLERS at daybreak, breakfasting at USNA Redoubt across the ANCRE, and taking over trenches just captured by two battalions of the 12th Division, the 7th Norfolks and the 9th Essex. Our front line (held by C and D Companies, with B in support and A in reserve), was SKYLINE TRENCH, and we had hardly got into position before an intense shelling of front and second lines began, and by the afternoon SKYLINE TRENCH was practically obliterated and very many casualties had been caused by our own as well as the enemy's heavies. At 9 p.m. shelling became more intense, and at 10 p.m. our depleted garrison, with hardly any officers or N.C.O.'s left, was attacked by two battalions of Guards, who penetrated a good deal of the front line, but failed to take the second line (RATION TRENCH). A small detachment of C Company on the right held out and defended from further attack about 200 yards of the front line, even extending this portion by bombing: their dogged resistence, continued until the whole trench was again taken twenty-four hours later, probably prevented the enemy from extending his gains,

Aug. 13

20 WAR RECORD OF THE

Aug. 14
An immediate bombing counter-attack by the local reserve failed, and a daylight attack by three companies of the BERKS was equally unsuccessful: the BUCKS Battalion relieved us in the afternoon and attacked at night, when the enemy abandoned the position without fighting.

Aug. 16
After two wet and unpleasant days in the ALBERT-BOUZINCOURT line, we again went up and held the shell holes on the site of SKYLINE TRENCH : shelling was fairly heavy but not so severe as before. On the second night the enemy showed signs of making another counter-attack; we sent this intelligence back, and, as we subsequently learned from prisoners captured, the attack was broken up and a number of casualties caused among the assembled attacking troops by our prompt artillery barrage.

Aug. 18
Two days in the line were followed by a peaceful day's bathing in the ANCRE opposite AVELUY, and two days back at BOUZINCOURT, where we again reorganised.

Aug. 21
Aug. 23
The next day saw us again at USNA redoubt and from here we relieved the 7th Worcesters North of OVILLERS. The battalion had a small front and was distributed in great depth. We improved our position by bombing attacks towards point 79, a much contested trench junction, and gained 30 yards. At night we dug a trench to connect our right and left companies. In the after-

Aug. 24
noon of next day we watched the successful afternoon attack by the 25th Division on LEIPZIC Redoubt on our left. The men by this time were getting tired and rather

Aug. 25
war worn, and a visit by the Divisional Commander to every post in and in front of the front line next day greatly cheered everyone. At night our patrols did good

work, and a Guards prisoner was taken. On the third
day we were relieved by the BERKS and went back to Aug. 26
RIBBLE STREET, and from here two companies were sent
up again to OVILLERS to support attacks by other
battalions in the brigade, and the remainder spent all
night carrying stores.

Then we left the line for bivouacs near BOUZINCOURT, Aug. 28
to find on arrival that they were already occupied : a
compromise was effected and we shared the accommodation.
Our next move was to wet and furnitureless huts Aug. 29
in BUS WOOD, where we were congratulated and encouraged
to further efforts by the Divisional Commander.

A week was spent at BUS, after which we took over a
peaceful sector of line in front of AUCHONVILLERS, look- Sept. 5
ing down on BEAUMONT HAMEL, only to return after three
days to better billets in BUS than before. Sept. 8

From BUS we marched back to BEAUVAL and spent a Sept. 11
pleasant week in our old billets, moving then to FIEN- Sept. 18
VILLERS where we stayed eleven days, did schemes
and were inoculated.

Another march through DOULLENS and the beautiful Sept. 29
country round LUCHEUX took us to good billets at WAR-
LUZEL.

We soon moved again to WARLINCOURT, where we Oct. 1
were accommodated in bad and crowded huts. No incident
marked our stay here except the adoption of
sandbag covers for our steel helmets and practices for
an attack, (never destined to materialise), on GOMME-
COURT WOOD, which was subsequently reconnoitred from Oct. 9
HEBUTERNE by officers.

> LE SARS.
> November
> and
> December
> 1916.

Oct. 19 — Eighteen days were spent at WARLINCOURT, and we then returned, in drenching rain, to inferior billets at WARLUZEL for a further three days, when we received orders to return to the SOMME.

Oct. 22
Oct. 23 — We marched back to BEAUVAL (fifth time), to TALMAS, and then, a long trek, to LAHOUSSOYE [24th] on the AMIENS-ALBERT road. After a week here and a limited
Oct. 31
Nov. 1 — amount of training, we moved to MILLENCOURT (just behind ALBERT) and next day to the wet muddy bivouacs between FRICOURT and CONTALMAISON, while senior officers went ahead to reconnoitre the SARS area.

Nov. 2 — On November 2nd we once more went into the line, after our longest spell on record in reserve, taking over the support area in front of MARTINPUICH from the 6th/7th Royal Scots Fusiliers (15th Division).

Surplus officers and five per cent. of the N.C.O.'s and men were left at ALBERT, and the transport were encamped at CHAPES SPUR (near LA BOISSELLE) where they were nearly isolated by a sea of mud.

Our position was on the forward slope of the hill in front of BAZENTIN, in full view from the BAPAUME ridge, but there was little shelling. Rations were for the first time brought up by pack ponies.

1/4th OXF. & BUCKS LT. INFTY.

After two days in support we went up to the front line on Nov. 4
the far side of LE SARS. The night was the blackest on
record, landmarks were few, a terrific rain-storm came
on : our guides, none too sure of their way in very
difficult country, lost the track, with the result that some
companies went through extraordinary adventures and
did not reach their positions for five hours.

We spent two days in unpleasant trenches and were
heavily shelled, companies relieving after 24 hours.

In reserve behind MARTINPUICH conditions were as Nov. 8
bad as in the front line, if not worse—disused water-
logged trenches, and a little corrugated iron-sheeting for
two companies, leaky cellars in MARTINPUICH for the remainder.

After three days work on accommodation here with scant Nov. 10
results, we were allotted BAZENTIN-LE-PETIT WOOD as a
rest area ; and by dint of bringing up all available
officers and men from behind, and scouring the neighbourhood for material of every description, tolerable
accommodation for the battalion was made before night-
fall.

In this camp, which for some reason was not
shelled, we spent a not unpleasant five days, finding small
working parties only. Then followed another cycle of two
days in support at MARTINPUICH and three days in the front Nov. 15
line at LE SARS. Conditions were as bad as possible— Nov. 17
hot food was not practicable, there was no shelter,
trenches were full of mud and water, and the overland
routes were very bad and heavily shelled at nights. In
consequence, on relief and arrival at PEAKE-WOOD- Nov. 20
CENTRE CAMP in the grey dawn, men were very ex-
hausted ; soup and the cheery attentions of the quarter-

master at VILLA STATION *en route* being the only bright features of an altogether unpleasant trek. The last batch of men who sailed with the battalion to go on leave will never forget the gradual transition from the waist-deep mud of the front line at LE SARS, across the shelled wilderness to MARTINPUICH, then back along the hopeless desolation of CONTALMAISON, to ALBERT; there to be finally speeded by shells from a long-range gun before the train got away and any idea could be entertained that the leave was a real thing.

Although everyone hated the mud even more than the shells, the mud had its uses, for it limited the destructive area of a 5·9 to a few yards, and more than one man has found himself after a burst lying literally on the lip of a crater.

Nov. 23 During five days back many of us went over to see and to exchange experiences with our second line battalion at OVILLERS.

Nov. 25 Our next trip to LE SARS passed without incident, except that we carried 48 hours' rations in with us, that subsequent rations were taken by limber to DESTREMONT FARM (just behind LE SARS), on the main ALBERT-BAPAUME road, an experiment which the transport will not soon forget, and that a patrol secured an important identification by capturing a prisoner of the Naval Division.

Nov. 29 After four days we marched back to the new camp of good Nissen huts at SCOTS' REDOUBT and spent five days
Dec. 4 here, four days at MIDDLE WOOD, and three days at
Dec. 8 SHELTER WOOD, all camps in the vicinity of Divisional Headquarters near CONTALMAISON.

Dec. 11 Our last tour at LE SARS was marked by a small raid

1/4th OXF. & BUCKS LT. INFTY. 25

on our post at the CHALK PIT almost immediately after our men had taken over, and our post thus caught at a disadvantage lost 4 killed, 2 wounded and 2 prisoners.

Rain, snow and sleet made conditions pretty hopeless, and our move back to SCOTS' REDOUBT after two days only was very welcome. — Dec. 12, Dec. 13

The next day we moved back to BECOURT CAMP, which consisted of good Nissen huts, and, but for the sea of mud everywhere, was very comfortable. — Dec. 14

We spent a good Christmas in the circumstances, and in spite of the arrival, two days before, of a draft of 200 Oxfordshire Hussars who were not allowed for in our Christmas rations. — Dec. 25

Leaving the SOMME area, we marched back to a cold and cheerless bell-tent camp at BRESLE (near BRAY), where we absorbed a draft of 50 Bucks Hussars and spent 12 days. — Dec. 28, Dec. 30

1917.

We next entrained at HEILLY, travelled to OISEMONT and spent three pleasant weeks in comfortable quarters at CERISY BULEUX, undergoing an easy period of training. — Jan. 9

> LA MAISONETTE.
> January 1917
> to
> March 1917.

After this we went up to the LA MAISONETTE area opposite PERONNE. The new small box respirators were issued at MARLY CAMP, FROISSY, where we first went into Divisional reserve. Brigade reserve was in SOPHIE TRENCH, HERBECOURT, and from here we went into the front line. The trenches taken over from the French — Jan. 29, Feb. 3, Feb. 7, Feb. 9

were not unlike our trenches at G sector HEBUTERNE: the dug-outs were mainly unfinished mineshafts, and there was practically no revetting: the distance from the enemy was small and we were worried a good deal with rifle grenades and "blue pigeons."

The next month was occupied in a regular cycle from front line to support in DESIREE VALLEY, to reserve at Camp 56, CAPPY, and then back again, the only incidents of special note being the tremendously heavy shelling of Battalion Headquarters and C Company in the FLAU-COURT sunken road, a return to G sector conditions after a thaw which made all trenches impassable, and contant rumours of the contemplated enemy retirement.

Feb. 15

Feb. 24

Feb. 25 As early as February 25th patrols investigated the enemy front line, only to find it held in strength, and on
Mar. 8 March 8th orders were issued for a two-company raid to ascertain how far the enemy's plans to withdraw had gone. After preliminary experiments with traversor
Mar. 17 mats, etc., and one postponement, the raid eventually took place, B and C Companies being sent up from Camp 56 by lorries on the previous evening.

The raid was entirely successful and the enemy was caught in the act of evacuating the front line, although a tremendous artillery activity during the night had almost led us to believe that he was go to attack. Our casualties only amounted to 1 killed and 4 wounded, and information of immense value was acquired.

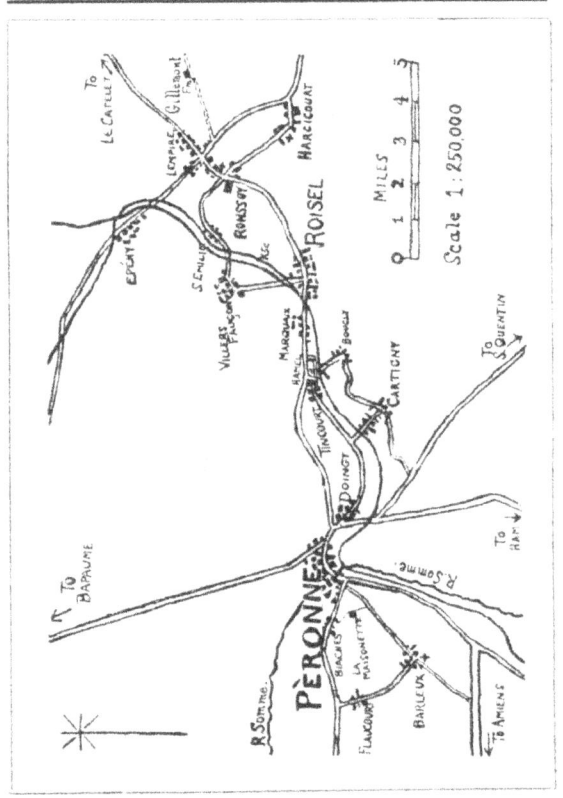

> PERONNE—RONSSOY
> ADVANCE.
> March and April,
> 1917.

      We then assiduously practised advanced guards and
Mar. 20 eventually left for PERONNE, crossing the SOMME by a
pontoon bridge at HALLE, and billeting in the wrecked
Mar. 21 and burning town. The next day was spent in making
roads round a large mine crater on the road between
Mar. 22 COURCELLES and DOINGT, and then we moved on to
CARTIGNY, where "WARD'S COLUMN," consisting of ourselves and the 5th Gloucesters, with a few guns, cyclists
and yeomanry, was instituted to follow up the retreating
enemy. The change from the torn country at LA
MAISONETTE, with its network of trenches, to the clean
rolling plains behind PERONNE, with mile upon mile of
pasture land and hardly a trench to be seen; the
advent of an entirely different form of warfare, were very
welcome and the spirits of everyone rose accordingly.

      C Company was put under cavalry orders and, as its
Mar. 23 first exploit, captured TINCOURT and HAMEL, while the
remainder of the Battalion was employed in clearing
roads. The German spirit of thoroughness was everywhere manifest: except at HAMEL, where a number of
civilians had been collected (who incidentally gave C
Company a tremendous reception), every habitable
building had been destroyed by exploding a mine or
large shell in the cellar; roads had been blocked by
felling the regular lines of poplars along their whole
length; the railway had been made useless by carrying

1/4th OXF. & BUCKS LT. INFTY.   29

away the line or blowing it up at every rail junction ; bridges and road junctions were blown up by mines ; telegraph lines were cut down. Much wanton damage too was visible everywhere—fruit trees sawn through, avenues of priceless trees destroyed for no purpose, even cemeteries rifled by some of the undisciplined troops left behind as rearguards.

C Company went on to MARQUAIX ; the large town of ROISEL was entered by D Company, who established a post in the east end, but were subsequently forced by weight of superior numbers to withdraw towards HAMELET: TINCOURT WOOD was cleared by 4 Battalion scouts. The remainder of the Battalion was kept at CARTIGNY in billets meanwhile and afterwards moved up to TINCOURT ; from here A and B carried out a scheduled attack on ROISEL, which we occupied, and Headquarters was moved to HAMEL. After this, to our regret, we were relieved by the Bucks and ordered back to billets at TINCOURT, where we spent a good deal of time in making cruciform posts. Our next move was to bad accomodation at MARQUAIX in bad weather, and from there to the outpost line facing RONSSOY by way of VILLERS-FAUCON and S. EMILIE. Very active patrol work was carried out and the enemy's position and strength carefully reconnoitred. — Mar. 24 / Mar. 25 / Mar. 26 / Mar. 27 / Mar. 29 / Apr. 3

At daybreak the Berks, the 5th Gloucesters and our- Apr. 5 selves carried out a highly successful attack on RONSSOY, and established a line at the east end of the village : the enemy was cleared out of RONSSOY before his arrangements to leave were complete, and many of the houses were found intact, with mines in process of being laid.

Our casualties were 7 killed and 24 wounded, and two

machine guns and many prisoners were captured.

At night we were relieved and went back to VILLERS-
Apr. 7 FAUCON, and thence two days later to a bivouac camp
Apr. 9 under the railway embankment, known as "K 5 central," where there was further activity with cruciform posts.
Apr. 13 We next moved up to the outpost line in front of RONSSOY for two days, back to the railway cutting at
Apr. 15 S. EMILIE for two days and then up again to the outpost
Apr. 17 line, C Company having been sent on to TOINE WOOD in advance.

On the left of our line was GILLEMONT FARM, which our patrols reported as being very strongly held: it was highly important that this strong point should be captured as it afforded the enemy his sole point of observation on our position, and by turning him out of it he would be compelled to occupy the low ground in front of the HINDENBERG line, which at this point was some 2,000 yards away and was overlooked by most of our front line posts.

Apr. 19 Accordingly D Company was ordered to attack the farm, and as previous operations had been successful with comparative ease, we were forbidden to employ any further troops except to exploit success. The attack was launched at 7 p.m. and met with resistance of the most determined character; the farm proved to be held very strongly and to be a nest of machine guns. We advanced the line 200 yards but failing to capture the farm were ordered to withdraw.

We were relieved the same night and marched back to HAMEL, where we spent a pleasant week, and the CURIOS performed in the open.

During this time other attacks were made on GILLE-

1/4th OXF. & BUCKS LT. INFTY.

MONT FARM, and, although a footing was obtained in the outbuildings, the enemy was never completely turned out of this strong point, which is to-day one of the worst shelled areas on the whole battle front.

We had one more "tour" in the neighbourhood of GILLEMONT, and then went back to "K 5 central," to HAMEL, and [May 2nd] to DOINGT CAMP, situated just east of PERONNE on the bank of the COLOGNE RIVER. — Apr. 27, Apr. 29, Apr. 30

> HERMIES—
> DEMICOURT.
> May and
> June 1917.

After ten days here we marched via PERONNE to COMBLES, being inspected *en route* by Lt.-General PULTENEY; the weather had become very hot and the march in steel helmets proved very trying. — May 12

We marched on, through unthinkably devastated country around SAILLY-SAILLISEL, to a camp at BEAULENCOURT, near BAPAUME, proceeding next day to the support line at HERMIES, which looked towards CAMBRAI in the distance. Our lines here consisted of a series of disconnected fire trenches, each capable of holding a post of a platoon in the front line and a half-platoon in the support line. No Man's Land varied greatly in width and the enemy's position west of the HINDENBURG line differed from day to day. The CANAL DU NORD ran through our lines on the right near HERMIES, and at one point we held one end of a demolished bridge while the enemy held the other some 20 yards away: the main BAPAUME-CAMBRAI road ran through the left of our — May 13, May 14 front north of DEMICOURT and here patrols wandered nearly a mile before encountering the enemy.

Events in the line here were on the whole pleasant, but not very noteworthy.

May 21 Patrolling was very active and a fighting patrol from HERMIES bayonetted and shot several of the enemy encountered in a post across the canal.

May 27 The visor attachment to the steel helmet for protecting the eyes was issued and withdrawn within a week. Gas projectors were experimented with and vast quantites of noxious vapours poured over enemy country without doing him much damage, as he nowhere held strongly a line which was so heavily protected by a canal and by three colossal belts of wire.

We went back to scattered support positions extending from DEMICOURT to BEAUMETZ, or to reserve behind VELU WOOD, where sports were held, and we held the front line at HERMIES or at DEMICOURT five times in all. On one occasion we dug, wired and occupied a new platoon post no less than four hundred yards in advance of our previous position without receiving any attention from the enemy, and on several occasions we carried out small daylight patrols in which the scouts secured good

June 6 information. During this period Lt.-Col. R. STEPHENS took over command from Major P. PICKFORD, M.C., who had commanded for a month in Lt.-Col. BARTLETT'S absence through illness.

July 2 Then came our march to the Headquarters designed for the fifth army at FREMICOURT, on to BIHUCOURT [3rd],

July 5 and so to BAILLEULMONT, where we first saw civilisation again after four months in the wilderness. Here we remained for 17 days undergoing fairly strenuous training for the great summer offensive in Flanders, in which we were destined to take part. Lectures on the prospective operations were given, and we carried out Brigade attacks on ADINFER WOOD over the trench-riddled country which was the front line before the enemy retired. Many of us went over to GOMMECOURT and visited spots which a year ago we had looked at for so long but from a distance only.

> YPRES.
> Aug. 1917
> to
> Oct. 1917.

Then we had an early morning move to MONDICOURT July 22 station and proceeded via HAZEBROUCK to GODEWARSVELDT, marching to fair billets, well behind the line, at HOUTKERQUE. Here Lt.-General SIR IVOR MAXSE, July 24 the Corps Commander, inspected us.

A week later we moved up to one of the many camps at S. JANS TER BIEZEN, close behind POPERINGHE, and July 30 on the following day the big attack began and was ex- July 31 traordinary successful for a start.

We next moved via POPERINGHE to tents at DAMBRE Aug. 4 CAMP, near VLAMERTINGHE, and on the following day relieved the 39th Division in the front line along the Aug. 5 STEENBEEK, sustaining many casualties in going up; and in three days without being called upon to attack we lost no less than 32 killed and 58 wounded from the intense shelling.

During a spell at DAMBRE CAMP Lt.-Col. BARTLETT, Aug. 9 D.S.O., again took over command, we again went up

c

Aug. 15 / Aug. 16 east of Ypres, assembled west of the STEENBEEK (with Battalion Headquarters at ALBERTA FARM), and attacked at dawn. The enemy put up a terrific resistance and we were unable to hit upon a satisfactory method of dealing with his concrete strong points, which were unaffected by our artillery barrage. We, however, gained a line just short of MON DU HIBOU and TRIANGLE FARM, an advance of about 500 yards. Next day we were sent
Aug. 17 back to DAMBRE CAMP, having lost 65 killed and 105 wounded, all company officers except two becoming casualties.
Aug. 27 After ten days we again moved up in the afternoon, to support an unsuccessful attack but were eventually used to relieve the advanced troops at night, and held the line
Aug. 28 for 24 hours, when the 58th Division took up the tale.
Aug. 29 We returned to DAMBRE CAMP and received large
Aug. 30 reinforcements at ROAD CAMP, S. JANS TER BIEZEN, where we carried out training and games as far as possible, and parties were taken to the seaside at MARDICK, near DUNKIRK, by lorry.
Sept. 16 Seventeen days later we entrained at ABEELE for AUDRUICQ and marched to BONNINGUES, a pretty little village not far from CALAIS, amid very fine country, the transport moving by road.

Here we carried out field-firing and battalion, brigade and divisional training. The weather was glorious and the time spent proved most enjoyable. The outstanding
Sept. 23 event was the Brigade Horse Show at LICQUES, in which we carried off the 1st and 2nd prizes for officers' chargers, the 1st and 2nd prizes for pack cobs, the 2nd prize for cookers, and three others for vehicles.
Sept. 24 A week at BONNINGUES was followed by a march to

ESTMONT and a train journey from WATTEN to BRIELEN Sept. 25
station (close to Ypres). From REIGERSBERG CAMP we Sept. 27
relieved the 58th Division, with Battalion Headquarters
at MON DU HIBOU. For three days we held the line
and carried out patrolling, the shelling being far less
severe than before, and after two days in support in Sept. 30
CANOPUS TRENCH and CALIFORNIA DRIVE, with Battalion Headquarters at CHEDDAR VILLA, we returned to
REIGERSBERG CAMP, C Company being bombed in Oct. 2
ADMIRAL'S ROAD (old "No Man's Land") on coming
out.

Later we were sent up to exploit the successful attack Oct. 4
of the 143rd Brigade, moving up to the ARBRE ridge in
the afternoon, but our orders were cancelled, and we remained in support. Two Companies were sent up to
reinforce the front line, and carried out good patrols to Oct. 6
VACHER FARM. Oct. 7

After another spell at DAMBRE CAMP in awful weather, Oct. 8
we went back to ROAD CAMP and thence from HOPOUTRE Oct. 12
Station (west of POPERINGHE) we entrained for LIGNY Oct. 14
S. FLOCHEL and marched to billets at CAUCOURT, in the
area behind the VIMY ridge. Oct. 15

From CAUCOURT we went to VILLERS-AU-BOIS, and Oct. 18
spent a fortnight training and footballing; here for the
first time our battalion band came into being.

We held the line in AVION (a suburb of LENS) for four Nov. 2
days, spent a similar period in support in VIMY village, Nov. 6
and then moved back to OTTAWA CAMP, MONT S. ELOI, Nov. 10
for another four days in reserve.

Our next move was back towards S. POL, and for a Nov. 14
week we billeted at SAVY, BERLES and VANDELICOURT,
small villages on the S. POL—LENS road. Here we lost

Major A. A. BRIDGEWATER, who had been with us throughout the whole campaign and who had done everything possible for our comfort and well-being for over 2½ years of active service as no other quartermaster ever did for any battalion.

ITALY.
Dec. 1917
to
March 1919.

Nov. 22 & 23   Then came rumours that we were to be sent to ITALY to assist the Italians in their attempt to stem the tide of invading Austrians, and we left SAVY on our long train journey south. The Battalion was divided into two train loads, the first going by way of MODANE and the MONT CENIS TUNNEL, the second along the RIVIERA via NICE, where a great welcome was accorded us by English and American residents. The journey, which took just over 5 days, was entirely novel, and as we reached the South of France the weather became gloriously warm and sunny, so that we were able to enjoy fully the grand scenery we passed through. We were taken by the first train to BOVELONE [28th] and after marching to CADEGLI OPPI [28th], and ALBAREDO [29th], we joined our second half battalion (who had detrained at CEREA [28th] and billetted at S. PIETRO DI MORUBIO [28th] and CASELLE

Nov. 30   [29th]), at ASIGLIANO.

Dec. 1   Then followed daily marches northward to AGUGLIARO [2nd], to MONTICELLA [3rd], to CAMPODORO and VILLA FRANCA [4th], to CAMPO S. MARTINO [5th], to PAVIOLA

[6th], until we finally found a resting place at TEZZE on Dec 14 the BRENTA, where we spent over a month.

By this time the Austrian offensive had been checked on the PIAVE by the Italians, and our immediate assistance did not seen likely to be required. The time was spent in reconnaissances of defence lines near BASSANO and of the foothills below the ASIAGO plateau, and in training and football. We were inspected by General Sir H. Plumer, the Commander in Chief, and by Dec. 5 Lt.-General Sir. R. Haking, the Corps Commander; we Dec. 21 fostered a warm entente with the French troops, and we discarded "oui" and "bon jour" in favour of "si" and "buon' giorno."

Our Christmas dinners of turkey, pork and plum Dec. 25 puddings were the best we had had since 1914, the weather was nearly always fine, and altogether we seemed to have struck "a very good war."

Then it was decided that the Division should be used on the PIAVE, and we began a march towards the Italian front through BOLZONELLA [24th], to BRUSAPORCO [26th] Jan. 24 (near CITTADELLA), where we halted for a week, then to Feb. 2 ALBAREDO, where we stayed 10 days, and on again Feb. 13 throngh ISTRANA to PORCELLENGO, where we again stayed a fortnight and whence the MONTELLO was reconnoitred. Our next move was to GIAVERA, and thence to Feb. 26 the front line [27th]; where we found ourselves holding a cliff 250 feet high with a line of posts pushed out on the foreshore of the PIAVE, at this point 1,500 yards wide. During our tour of four days patrols were sent to GENOVA Island, and several attempts were made to ford the main channel of the PIAVE, in order to get in touch with the enemy, but these were frustrated by the current. We

Mar. 3	then went back to the reserve battalion area at BAVARIA, where the accommodation consisted of dry and roomy house billets, as it did even in the front line; in fact so peaceful and comfortable a sector we had never yet seen.
Mar. 7	In our next and last visit to the PIAVE front line we succeeded in getting one man of a patrol on to the enemy's side of the river, and a post was located and fired a VEREY light from about 100 yards away, but unfortunately the temperature of the water reduced patrols to too cold a state to achieve anything. We were then relieved at BAVARIA by Italian troops, and marched back, via
Mar. 15	CUSIGNANA and PORCELLENGO [15th], TORRESELLI [16th]
Mar. 18	and PALAZZO BRESSANIN [17th], to ARSEGO. From this place we sent three representatives to the Inter-Allied Sports at ROME to compete in the British Tug-of-War Team.
Mar. 23	Five days later we moved to S. MARIA DI NON, where training was continued for another ten days and
Mar. 31	some good sports were held.
Apr. 2	Then we had a long march down to GALZIGNANO on the COLLI EUGANEI, near PADOVA, which had been acquired by G.H.Q. as a training area for the mountains, where it was proposed to use the British and French troops during the hot season.
	We carried out a novel and interesting fortnight's training, practising hill-climbing, attacks through smoke screens, and the use of pack mules in hill warfare.
Apr. 16	Then we started our long trek to the ASIAGO PLATEAU by way of SARMEGO [16th] MONTECCHIO MAGGIORE [17th] CASTELGOMBERTO [18th] (where we stayed three days and officers were sent up to reconnoitre the "line of the hills" and the "intermediate line," defence systems

between the Plateau and the Plain), S. MARIA, near Apr. 21
SARCEDO [21st], MARE and VALLE DI SOPRA [22nd]. Here
we began the serious climb up the mountains, and reconnaissances of the front line and the GRANEZZA neighbourhood were made.

Pack transport was increased by twenty animals.
Echelon A was established at GRANEZZA on the Plateau
and Echelon B at FARA in the Plain. A half-way house
was adopted at SCIESSERE, to which Echelon B animals
drew the rations, Echelon A carrying forward to
GRANEZZA, and pack animals on to the front line.

On April 29th we marched up by mule track to Apr. 29
GRANEZZA, accomplishing the climb in 2½ hours, and on
the following day we took over the front line at S. SISTO, Apr. 30
facing ASIAGO.

The situation here was, from a military point of view,
a doubtful one: the Austrian was within 2½ miles of
the ridge of mountains south of GRANEZZA which dominated the whole of the Venetian plain from VENICE to
VERONA, and it was realised that if he once reached this
ridge, lines below this could only temporarily check his
advance, and a retirement to the ADIGE or the Po became
necessary.

In this narrow strip of mountain running down to the
edge of the plateau, where our front line was, and fed by
only two roads, were concentrated practically all our
guns, our support and reserve troops, all our stores,
our ammunition, and our Echelon A transport.

Happily a thick pine forest concealed all our dispositions
and movement, or the position would have been
untenable.

No Man's Land, about a mile wide, began where the

forest ended : the plateau was over two miles wide and on the far side rose higher mountains than on our side. But the enemy, whose main position lay, like ours, on the edge of the plateau, had decided to include ASIAGO, and so held a line through the middle of the plateau, which was entirely without cover, which was completely dominated by our position, and which could be pounded at will, with excellent observation, by our guns.

What chiefly impressed us in Italian military engineering were the marvellous roads, in excellent order, up impossible precipices; the wonderful trenches bored through the solid rock (but without any dug-outs as we knew them); and the *telefericas* which carried ammunition, rations, and even men, from the plain to the mountains in about half-an-hour, whereas the winding roads took a lorry perhaps two hours to reach the same point.

Apr. 30   When first we arrived we found things very peaceful; hardly a shell was ever fired and patrolling was practically unknown. Within a fortnight we changed all this; our guns began to make the enemy's positions very uncomfortable, and as usual we undertook active patrolling. The weather became fine and warm, and our support quarters—in Italian bivouacs—became tolerable, if not very proof against enemy retaliation. Three weeks in the line and in support passed without much incident, except

May 14   for a raid on an enemy advanced post, in which we succeeded in bringing in a prisoner, who had an accident with a bomb and killed himself just as he was being brought into our line.

May 19   The 23rd Division relieved us and we marched back via MARE [20th] and S. MARIA [21st] to BROGLIANO [22nd]. Here we were in fairly comfortable quarters and carried out

the usual training and range-firing. We were issued with
sun helmets and khaki drill, of which we later found the May 26
need in the plain.

On our return to the plateau we went to the left May 30
Division front at BOSCON by way of S. DONA [1st] and June 3
SERONA [2nd], at first going into support on M. LEMERLE
[3rd], and then into the line opposite CANOVE. Here we June 9
held the line by outpost platoons pushed well in advance
of the front line at night, and by forward observation
posts by day: the country in front of the front line was
greatly intersected by ravines, which, on an extended
front, were practically impossible to watch properly.

An enemy strong point—VAISTER FARM—in front of
his front line, was a stumbling block in the way of patrol
work and inconsistent with our aims of having complete
command of No Man's Land; it was therefore appropriat- June 13
ed and held.

On the night of June 14th general information from June 14
deserters and prisoners indicated that the great Austrian
offensive was to begin on the following morning, but it
was not expected that we should be involved except in
the bombardment. A prisoner, captured by us at midnight in a small raid, was understood by signs to say that
a heavy attack was to be made on us after a terrific
bombardment with gas and H.E. beginning at 3 a m.
He was hurried back to Divisional Headquarters with
the information, and all precautions were taken.

| AUSTRIAN ATTACK. |

Punctually at 3 a.m. a most tremendous bombardment June 15

began with a salvo of 8″ shells over Divisional Headquarters, and the gassing of batteries and the one road of approach to our sector of the front line. An enormous shell dump was blown up at HANDLEY CROSS, the cross roads past which all traffic to our sector must come ; and our communications forward from Battalion Headquarters were all destroyed in the first five minutes and backwards in the first 45 minutes. The actual attack was made shortly before 7 a.m., and, as identified by prisoners captured, no less than seven battalions were involved in the attack on our front : the front on our right, which had a very exposed approach, was intended to be turned by a flanking movement. The front on our left was pierced and a wedge driven in. Our front companies, after putting up a great fight in the outpost line, where the small garrison found itself surrounded, contested every inch of ground, but were engaged in rear by enemy who had filtered through on their left, and towards noon were compelled to withdraw fighting to the neighbourhood of Battalion Headquarters.

Meanwhile an improvised semi-circular defence had been made on a small ridge around Battalion Headquarters, which was in a sunken road some 500 yards behind the front line ; and after our local reserves and our headquarters company had delivered two counter attacks without succeeding in restoring the front line, this line of rocks and bits of trenches was manned by the surviving clerks, orderlies, servants, cooks, &c. These men held out all day against repeated attacks, despite the fact that the enemy had got machine-guns into position level with headquarters on the right, 200 yards away in front, and 500 yards behind on the left. Later in the day

1/4th OXF. & BUCKS LT. INFTY. 43

our depleted garrison was reinforced by the Berks, and
at dawn next morning, following close on a Stokes-mortar June 16
barrage, we and the Berks counter-attacked, to find the
enemy in the act of retreating in considerable disorder,
leaving hundreds of dead and wounded ; and we were
able by 7 a.m. to restore our original line and to send
patrols into No Man's Land. The day's fighting had cost
us six officers and 42 other ranks killed, two officers and
92 other ranks wounded, besides 34 men cut off and
made prisoners, but we succeeded in breaking up the
whole attack, and taking several hundred prisoners and
many mountain guns, machine guns, flammenwerfers
(used in getting through our wire), and other war
material. The aim of the Austrian attack, as we afterwards learned, was very ambitious, and our obstinate
resistance, which prevented him from extending the gap
he had made, probably succeeded in stopping a manœuvre
which might have led to the ultimate evacuation of the
mountains and retirement into the plains.

Following upon our hard fighting we moved back to June 16
CARRIOLA, behind Divisional Headquarters, when we had
time to realise that we had a severe epidemic of so-called
" mountain fever," no less than 67 cases being sent to
hospital in four days.

During this period the Division sustained a very heavy
blow in the loss of Major-General Sir R. FANSHAWE,
K.C.B., who handed over the command to Major-General June 20
Sir H. B. WALKER, K.C.B , after commanding us for
over three years, during which time he had endeared
himself to all ranks, especially of the Oxfordshire Battalion,
by his intensity of purpose, his unfailing consideration
for the men, his total disregard for his personal safety and

comfort, and his marked interest in the battalion of his own regiment serving under him.

His farewell message was :—"On handing over the command of the Division I wish to thank all units for their devotion. I feel the parting so deeply that I will not say more than wish the Division collectively success under their new commander, and all ranks individually success during the remainder of the war and after it is over."

June 22 We spent a peaceful week at MARZIELE, a bivouac camp pitched on the steep southern slope of the mountains, commanding the most glorious view from VENICE to PADOVA and VICENZA, but with no possibilities for recreation.

July 1 We then revisited BROGLIANO for 17 days, where we did tactical schemes and held sports. We returned to the
July 17 ASIAGO front by intensely hot night-marches, following days of almost intolerable heat, with a never-to-be-forgotten stage for 18 hours only at CLUB CAMP (4,500 feet
July 19 up), after our climb of the mountains. Incidents of this
July 25 tour were the capture of four Bosnians in POSLEN GULLY on the left of GUARDINALTI ridge, where our outposts were, and several patrols to S. AVE, a farm within 100 yards of the enemy's front line.

July 30 After a rest in CLUB CAMP we again took over
Aug. 7 the line, three Italians escaping from ASIAGO into our lines after extraordinary experiences as prisoners.

Aug. 18 An uneventful tour in the front line opposite MORAR, a spell in support disturbed by the institution of artillery "crashes" by guns of all calibres at stated hours and usually replied to by the enemy, and a pleasant time at
Aug. 25 MARZIELE camp with daily concerts by our own band, brought us to September.

A period of almost nightly raids then began. It was found that the enemy was getting demoralised by our activity, and it was desirable that this state of affairs should be fostered, so raids, at first by platoons, and later by companies and battalions, were ordered. In September we were selected to raid the enemy front line at Sec on the out-skirts of ASIAGO, on a front of 1,000 yards to a depth of 400 yards. We were taken out of the front line to train for the operation; an excellent model of the area was prepared by the scouts, platoons were lectured at the model on their exact task and were then shown the ground from an observation post; patrols were made each night so that everyone knew the lie of the land, and officers were taken to artillery O.P.s to study the country in detail. The raid took place at 4 a.m. with a barrage from 100 guns. A searchlight was used, and a demonstration was made on AVE further to the left. Everything went exactly according to plan: one officer and 37 prisoners and three machine guns were captured, our own casualties amounting to ten in all.

Sept. 6

Sept. 10

The following day we returned to the line and oscillated between reserve at GRANEZZA, support at KABEBLABA, and front line at POSLEN or S. SISTO, until the end of October, when a BUCKS raid produced the information that the enemy had evacuated his much shelled line south of ASIAGO and retired to the foot of the mountains opposite.

Sept. 11

Oct. 29

SEC RAID

> ADVANCE INTO AUSTRIA.

Our scouts were in ASIAGO Station about 6 hours after the raid, and reported ASIAGO clear of the enemy (incidentally they were the first Allied troops to enter the town) and a portion of A Company was sent over to the old front line to support them. Our patrol pushed forward and got into touch with the enemy on his new line, and the BERKS were ordered to establish forward posts in front of ASIAGO, after which our patrols were withdrawn.

Oct. 31 Two nights later the French on our right raided the enemy's front line, found it evacuated and decided to attack next morning.

Nov. 1 Our Division co-operated, sending the BUCKS and BERKS to attack the M. CATZ line at 5 40 a.m. We left our trenches and assembled in ASIAGO at 8 a.m. in support of this attack, in which the BUCKS were completely successful in taking M. CATZ itself on the right, though on the left, towards the VAL D'ASSA, the enemy facing the BERKS put up a determined rearguard fight all day.

We followed the BUCKS, intending to work round the rear of the obstinate enemy on the left. We reached ROCCOLO N.E. on the slopes of M. INTEROTTO as it got dark, and A and B Companies were sent on to find outposts and to link up between the BUCKS and the BERKS.

Nov. 2 Next day we were sent to M. MEATTA above the VAL D'ASSA to guard the passage of the 143rd Brigade into AUSTRIA, and later we moved for the night down to VALLE DI PORTULE.

We then advanced up the VAL D'ASSA in column of Nov. 3
route, meeting thousands of prisoners and incidentally
persuading a battalion and a half, who had been overlooked, to surrender to our Headquarters Company at
CALDONAZZO. This march of over 25 miles, lasting from
4.30 a.m. to 5 p m. with only one halt of three quarters
of an hour was a very noteworthy performance, following
as it did upon two very hard days marching, fighting and
outpost work, and 12 days in the line ; only the wonderful spirits of the men enabled them to carry on with no
straggling or falling out. Here we guarded prisoners and
stores, fed civilians, etc., for 4 days, sending A and C
Companies back as prisoner escorts to ASIAGO.

Then followed the most trying march of over 50 miles Nov. 9
back to the plains, to VEZZENA [9th], to VALLE DI
PORTULE [10th], through the ruins of ASIAGO, where our
band met us, to GRANEZZA [11th], to THIENE [12th],
and finally to MAGLIO DI SOPRA, which we reached Nov. 13
two days after the signing of the armistice with Germany.

At MAGLIO two composite companies of the Battalion Dec. 16
represented the brigade at a review by the Italian Corps
Commander, and we were inspected as a Brigade by our Dec. 18
Divisional Commander. On December 23rd the first 1919
demobilisation train, and on February 25th the last de- Feb. 25
mobilisation train left, and gradually the Battalion was
whittled down to its cadre of 4 officers and 47 other
ranks who finally left ITALY on March 24th, and reached Mar. 24
ENGLAND on March 30th. Mar. 30

On our return to OXFORD the Battalion was accorded a civil reception before being finally dispersed,
after a period of almost exactly four years' service overseas.

APPENDIX.

Extracts from Official Despatches, &c.

From list of Battalions mentioned in General French's First Despatch dated 19.5.16 :—

"1/4th Battalion Oxfordshire and Buckinghamshire Light Infantry."

From Sir Douglas Haig's Despatch dated 18.3.17 :—

"Our patrols were so close upon the heels of the Germans at LA MAISONETTE that they caught them in trenches they were preparing to evacuate and did much execution by a bombing attack, taking a fair number of prisoners in the dug-outs."

From Sir Douglas Haig's Despatch dated 7.4.17 :—

"We have captured RONSSOY and BASSE BOULOGNE after sharp fighting in which we took 22 prisoners and three machine guns. The retreating enemy was caught in his own wire entanglements and suffered heavily under our machine-gun fire."

Farewell letter from General H. Rawlinson, Commanding 4th Army, dated 22.5.17 :—

"I cannot allow the 48th Division to leave the 4th Army after seven months' strenuous service without expressing to all ranks my appreciation and warm thanks for the valuable services they have rendered. After a winter of unexampled severity in indifferent trenches, the change to open warfare in March and April found them in a high state of efficiency.

"The skilful leadership and dash displayed in the capture of PERONNE, SEMILIE, EPEHY, BASSE-BOULOGNE

[RONSSOY] and TOMBOIS and GILLEMONT FARMS are deserving of the highest praise and show that the standard of efficiency that has been reached, more especially in the close combination of artillery and infantry, is an exceedingly high one.

" I congratulate all ranks on the successes they have attained and I shall look forward to some future date when I trust I may have the good fortune to find the Division once more under my command."

Farewell letter from General H. de la P. Gough, Commanding 5th Army, dated 14.10.17 :—

"The 48th Division have taken part in much hard fighting during the past two months including five general engagements. Their spirit and determination on all occasions have been admirable and temporary set backs have in no way affected their morale. I am very sorry to bid good-bye to such a dependable Division and feel sure that the future holds many further successes for them."

From G.O.C.-in-C.'s [Italy] dated 15.6.18 :—

The British front (held by four Battalions) was attacked by four Austrian Divisions. On the right the attack completely failed with very heavy losses to the enemy. On the left the enemy penetrated our front line on a front of some 2,500 yards to a maximum depth of about 1,000 yards, where he has been firmly contained all day. The enemy has suffered very heavy losses."

" 16.6.18. The pocket on the British Front, mentioned in my communique of last night has been cleared of the enemy during the night and early hours of the morning, and we are now again established in our original front line. Over 350 prisoners have been counted and we have in addition captured two mountain guns and a considerable number of machine guns."

" 17.6.18. The enemy is re-organising after his severe defeat. Captured maps show that his objectives were very ambitious and included the capture of MONTE PAU and CIMA DI FONTE. [Nearly five miles behind our outpost line.]

"The number of prisoners has increased to 716, including 12 officers. The total amount of captured material actually brought in is four mountain guns, 43 machine guns, and seven flammenwerfers."

1/4th OXF. & BUCKS LT. INFTY.   51

"19.6.18. The number of prisoners taken by us now exceeds a thousand. Captured material now amounts to five mountain guns, 72 machine guns, 20 flammenwerfers, and one trench mortar, and further material remains to be collected."

From Despatch of G.O.C.-in-C. British Troops, Italy, dated 18.6.18:—

"I should like to draw particular attention to the fighting qualities displayed by the following regiments in the battle of the 15th inst.:—Northumberland Fusiliers, Sherwood Foresters, Royal Warwicks, Oxfordshire and Buckinghamshire Light Infantry."

From General Diaz, Italian Army Despatch of 18.6.18:—

"For the great days of June 15th and 16th the following units merit special mention as the exponents of the valour of all the others:—Northumberland Fusiliers, Sherwood Foresters, Royal Warwicks, and Oxfordshire and Buckinghamshire Light Infantry."

From Italian Official Despatch, dated 11.9.18:—

"On the ASIAGO Plateau British troops effected a brilliant coup-de-main inflicting considerable losses on the enemy in a fierce hand-to-hand struggle and capturing seventy-seven prisoners, eight machine guns, and abundant war material. [Two other British Battalions raided the Austrian lines on the same night.]"

Message from G.O.C. 48th Division to G.O.C. 145th Brigade, dated 10.9.18:—

"I congratulate you, Major Pickford, and the Oxfords on last night's successful raid against SEC.—Major-General Walker."

Despatch from General the Earl of Cavan, K.P., K.C.B., M.V.O., C.-in-C. British Forces in Italy, dated 15.11.18.:—

"The 48th Division under Major-General Sir H. B. Walker, K.C.B., D.S.O., has remained on the ASIAGO Plateau, forming part of the Sixth Italian Army. . . . On 30.10.18 patrols pushed beyond ASIAGO found the enemy rearguards in position on the line M. CATZ—BOSCO—CAMPOROVERE. . . . At 5.45 a.m. on 1.11.18 an attack was launched against this line and M. CATZ was captured. . . . On the morning of 2.11.18 the success gained by the 145th Infantry Brigade was wisely exploited. M. MOSCIAGH was captured . . . and the advance became more rapid and by dark the advanced guards had reached VEZZENA, and thus set foot on Austrian soil. The Division was, therefore, the first British Division to enter enemy territory on the Western Front.

" On the morning of 3.11.18 the advance was again resumed, and by dark both CALDONAZZO and LEVICO had been occupied. . . . The captures in prisoners and guns made by the 48th Division cannot be accurately ascertained. They amounted to at least 20,000 prisoners and 500 guns. Included amongst the prisoners were the Commander of the 3rd Corps and three Divisional Commanders.

"It must be remembered that this division was attacking very formidable mountain positions with only a fifth part of the artillery that would have been at its disposal had the initial attack started on the ALTIPIANO.

" Its performance, therefore, in driving in the enemy's rearguards so resolutely, while climbing up to heights of 5,000 feet, is all the more praiseworthy."

SUMMARY OF CASUALTIES.

	Killed.		Wounded.		Prisoners.		
	Officers	Other Ranks	Officers	Other Ranks	Officers	Other Ranks	Total.
BELGIUM.							
PLOEGSTEERT (Trenches)	2	11	3	45	–	–	61
FRANCE.							
HEBUTERNE (Trenches)	7	33	1	98	–	1	140
ALLOUAGNE (Bomb Accident)	1	2	–	7	–	–	10
POZIERES (Sickle Trench, 19.7.16 Attack)	–	20	2	81	–	–	103
,, (,, 23.7.16, Attack)	5	73	8	166	–	–	252
,, (Sky-Line Trench, 14.8.16 German Attack)	3	50	5	94	–	–	152
,, (,, 16.8.16—26.8.16 Trenches)	–	20	1	62	–	–	83
AUCHONVILLERS (Trenches)	–	–	–	3	–	–	3
LE SARS (Trenches)	1	25	3	93	–	2	124
LA MAISONETTE (Trenches)	1	6	2	16	–	–	25
PERONNE-RONSSOY (Attack)	–	24	2	48	–	2	76
GILLEMONT FARM (Attack)	1	18	1	43	–	–	63
HERMIES AND DEMICOURT (Trenches)	–	7	–	31	–	2	40
BELGIUM.							
YPRES (5.8.17—8.8.17, Trenches)	2	30	3	55	–	–	90
,, (16.8.17—17.8.17, Attack)	5	72	5	93	–	–	175
,, (27.8.17—28.8.17)	–	10	–	18	–	–	28
,, (27.9.17—10.10.17, Trenches)	1	13	–	40	–	–	54
FRANCE.							
VIMY (Trenches)	–	3	–	21	–	–	24
ITALY.							
ASIAGO PLATEAU (15.5.18—19.5.18 8.8.18—11.10.18, Trenches)	–	5	1	13	–	–	19
,, (Austrian Attack)	6	48	2	85	–	39	180
,, (Raid on SEC.)	–	4	1	6	–	1	12
Killed in Action while attached to other Units (various dates)	–	11	–	–	–	–	11
Died on Active Service	1	12	–	–	–	–	13
Total	36	497	40	1118	0	47	1738

WAR RECORD OF THE

Roll of Officers, Non-Commissioned Officers and Men KILLED IN ACTION.

NOTE.—Officers and Men in subsequent Lists who have lost their lives on Active Service are marked with an asterisk (*) before the name.

Regtl. No.	Rank.	Name.	Coy.		Date.	Place of Burial.
PLOEGSTEERT, 8.4.15—19.6.15							
2610	Pte.	White, J. H. R.	C		11.4.15	Ploegsteert
3107	Pte.	Strong, M.	B		27.4.15	,,
273	Sgt.	Boneham, W.	C		8.5.15	,,
1811	Pte.	Partridge, H.	A		9.5.15	,,
	Capt.	DASHWOOD, E. G.	B		12.5.15	,,
2604	Pte.	Sharman, F.	C		23.5.15	,,
1790	Pte.	Butler, A. G.	D		27.5.15	,,
	2/Lt.	HERMON-HODGE, J.P.	D		25.5.15	,,
4926	R.S.M.	Adams, A. S.		Wounded	29.5.15	
				Died	13.6.15	Boulogne
2334	Pte.	Hill, G. T. B.	D		30.5.15	Ploegsteert
1387	L/C.	Mitchell, F.	D		14.6.15	,,
655	Pte.	Smith, S. W.	B		17.6.15	,,
1934	Pte.	Huggonson, J.	D		18.6.15	,,
ALLOUAGNE (Bomb Accident), 12.7.15.							
	Lt.	VYNER, C. J. S.	A	Wounded	12.7.15	
				Died	24.7.15	Lillers
2748	Pte.	Harris, A. G.	C	Wounded	12.7.15	
				Died	13.7.15	,,
2304	Pte.	Joynes, A. T.	B		12.7.15	Allouagne
HEBUTERNE, 20.7.15—16.7.16.							
2360	Pte.	Whitlock, E.	C		22.7.15	Hebuterne
962	Pte.	Castle, A. E.	C		30.7.15	,,
2780	Pte.	Wiblin, A. G.	B	Wounded	8.8.15	
				Died	22.8.15	Bristol

1/4th OXF. & BUCKS LT. INFTY. 55

HEBUTERNE—continued.

Regtl. No.	Rank	Name.	Coy.		Date.	Place of Burial.
1958	Pte.	Culverwell, R.	D	Wounded	17.8.15	
				Died	17.8.15	Louvencourt
1667	Pte.	Searle, G. A. E.	D		24.9.15	Hebuterne
2311	Pte.	Wheeler, J. J.	D	Wounded	24.9.15	
				Died	25.9.15	Louvencourt
2682	Pte.	Brooks, F. S.	A	Wounded	27.9.15	
				Died	5.10.15	Rouen
	Capt.	Treble, J. N.	D		18.10.15	Hebuterne
1930	L/C.	Ruddle, A.	D	Wounded	18.10.15	
				Died	19.10.15	Louvencourt
3605	Pte.	Timms, A. W.	C		19.10.15	Hebuterne
2944	Pte.	Broome, J.	B	(Accdtly)	3.12.15	,,
2649	Pte.	Dolley, A. T.	B	(Accdtly)	3.12.15	,,
3080	Pte.	Johnson, A. E.	B	(Accdtly)	3.12.15	,,
3117	Pte.	Witchell, E.	B	(Accdtly)	3.12.15	,,
981	Pte.	Taylor, H. A.	C	Died	14.12.15	Villers Bocage
	Lt.	Doyne, P. D.	A		28.12.15	Hebuterne
2337	L/C.	Faulkner, W. H.	A	Wounded	29.12.15	
				Died	30.12.15	Louvencourt
2409	L/C.	Howkins, W. J.	A		31.12.15	Hebuterne
2712	Pte.	Adams, S.	A		31.12.15	,,
3527	Pte.	Tyrell, C. G.	A		31.12.15	,,
1301	Pte.	Pratley, E. W.	B		12.1.16	,,
	Capt. & Adjt.	Griffin, I. E.		Wounded	11.2.16	
				Died	12.2.16	Beauval
7119	R.S.M.	Pearce, E. J.			11.2.16	Hebuterne
2659	Pte.	Alexander, P.	C	Wounded	11.2.16	
				Died	12.2.16	Beauval
2399	L/C.	Wake, A. T.	B		23.3.16	Hebuterne
2239	Pte.	Walton, J.	B	Wounded	26.3.16	
				Died	9.4.16	Beauval
3046	Cpl.	Wyatt, C. J.	A	Wounded	9.4.16	
				Died	10.4.16	,,
4890	Pte.	Long, S.	D	Wounded	9.4.16	
				Died	15.4.16	Etretat
	2/Lt.	Hughes, T. D.	A		3.5.16	Hebuterne
	2/Lt.	King, J. S. C., D.C.M.	C		3.5.16	,,
1701	Sgt.	Barnes, W.	B	Wounded	3.5.16	
				Died	3.5.16	,,
4486	Pte.	Tolley, A.	C		5.5.16	,,

56 WAR RECORD OF THE

HEBUTERNE—continued.

Regtl. No.	Rank.	Name.	Coy.		Date.	Place of Burial.
2937	Pte.	Bennett, E. L.	B	Wounded	7.5.16	Hebuterne
				Died	7.5.16	,,
2379	Pte.	Waine, F.	A	Died	14.5.16	Villers Bocage
	Major	HADDEN, E. W. R.		Died	11.6.16	Abbeville
	Capt.	GRICE T. G. (Scottish R.)		Wounded	13.6.16	
				Died	15.6.16	Couin
1617	Pte.	Smith, W. N.	A		13.6.16	Hebuterne
3001	Pte.	Telfer, J.	A		5.7.16	,,
2641	L/C.	Tarrant, O. E.	B	Wounded	10.7.16	,,
				Died	10.7.16	,,
4997	Pte.	Mayo, F.	D		10.7.16	,,
	2/Lt.	RAWLINSON, G. M.	C	Wounded	14.7.16	
				Died	16.7.16	Couin
1303	Cpl.	Checkley, C.	C		14.7.16	Not known
4897	Pte.	Cox, W. A.	C		14.7.16	Hebuterne

POZIERES (SICKLE TRENCH)—19.7.16.

2256	C.S.M.	Fincher, E. F.	A		19.7.16	Pozieres
1431	Sgt.	Brooks, P.	C		19.7.16	,,
1733	Sgt.	Cook, A.	B		19.7.16	,,
2599	L/C.	Plester, W. H.	C		19.7.16	,,
2941	Pte.	Bolton, G. L.	A		19.7.16	,,
3300	Pte.	Bryant, H.	B		19.7.16	,,
1874	Pte.	Checkley, H.	C	Wounded	19.7.16	
				Died	20.7.16	Davours
5075	Pte.	Crawford, E.	B		19.7.16	Pozieres
1592	Pte.	Field, T. A. G.	B	Wounded	19.7.16	
				Died	24.7.16	Puchevillers
2774	Pte.	Hicks, R. T.	B		19.7.16	Pozieres
2679	Pte.	Mitchell, T. F.	A		19.7.16	,,
5274	Pte.	Prior, F. W.	A		19.7.16	,,
4901	Pte.	Rawlings, A.	C		19.7.16	,,
3685	Pte.	Sherborne, F.	B	Wounded	19.7.16	
				Died	20.7.16	Warloy-Baillon
2365	Pte.	Slay, F. W.	A		19.7.16	Pozieres
4750	Pte.	Smith, L.	C		19.7.16	,,
5109	Pte.	Taylor, D.	C	Wounded	19.7.16	
				Died	1.8.16	Heilly

1/4th OXF. & BUCKS LT. INFTY.

POZIERES—continued.

Regtl. No.	Rank.	Name.	Coy		Date.	Place of Burial.
2609	Pte.	Timms, G. W.	C		19.7.16	Pozieres
3418	Pte.	Townsend, W.	B		19.7.16	,,
5211	Pte	Young, R. W.	A		19.7.16	,,

POZIERES (SICKLE TRENCH)—23.7.16.

Regtl. No.	Rank.	Name.	Coy		Date.	Place of Burial.
	Capt.	BLAKE, J. E.	D		23.7.16	Pozieres
	Capt.	BROOKS, B. B. B.	B		23.7.16	,,
	2/Lt.	FRIEAKE, G. M.	D	Wounded	23.7.16	
				Died	1.8.16	Rouen
	2/Lt.	HALL, T.N.	B	Wounded	23.7.16	
				Died	15.8.16	,,
	2/Lt.	HUTCHINS, D. M. (5th Middlesex)	C.	Wounded	23.7.16	
				Died	2.8.16	Beauval
1654	C.S.M.	Peet, J. T., M.M.	D		23.7.16	Pozieres
1776	Sgt.	Barlow, T. P., M.M.	D		23.7.16	,,
1897	Sgt.	Herbert, J. H.	D	Wounded	23.7.16	
				Died	27.7.16	Rouen
2488	Sgt.	Newman, F., M.M.	C	Wounded	23.7.16	
				Died	25.8.17	Adderbury, England
1808	Sgt.	Price. O.	A		23.7.16	Pozieres
1359	Sgt.	Smith, N.	A		23.7.16	,,
1492	Sgt.	Wilks, M. B.	B		23.7.16	,,
2786	Cpl.	Harris, S. C.	A		23.7.16	,,
3061	Cpl.	Jones, D.	A		23.7.16	,,
1942	Cpl.	Newman, H.	D		23.7.16	,,
2851	Cpl.	Saunders, H. F.	B		23.7.16	,,
3443	Cpl.	Turner, G.	B		23.7.16	,,
2801	L/C.	Bunce, H.	A		23.7.16	,,
3052	L/C.	Draper, W. H.	A		23.7.16	,,
2842	L/C.	Finch, C. H.	A		23.7.16	,,
3555	L/C.	Fisher, J. W.	D		23.7.16	,,
3611	L/C.	Gray, L.	D		23.7.16	,,
2163	L/C.	Green, W.	D		23.7.16	,,
3210	L/C.	Long, A. C.	B		23.7.16	,,
2622	L/C.	Long, H. E.	B		23.7.16	,,
4994	L/C.	Piper, F.	A		23.7.16	,,
2511	L/C.	Rivers, H. S.	C		23.7.16	,,
2624	L/C.	Tarrant, E. W.	B	Wounded	23.7.16	
				Died	1.8.16	Rouen

58 WAR RECORD OF THE

POZIERES—continued.

Regtl. No.	Rank.	Name.	Coy.	Date.	Place of Burial.
1915	L/C.	Tustain, M.	C	23.7.16	Pozieres
3469	Bglr.	Green, G.	C	23.7.16	,,
3005	Bglr.	Rogers, C.	B	23.7.16	,,
3514	Pte.	Arkell, F.	A	23.7.16	,,
4333	Pte.	Baker, G.	C	23.7.16	,,
5165	Pte.	Barson, J.	B	23.7.16	,,
2639	Pte.	Bartlett, A. H.	A	23.7.16	,,
4155	Pte.	Blundell, A. H.	D	23.7.16	,,
2095	Pte.	Bolton, J.	C	23.7.16	,,
1823	Pte.	Busby, B. S. G.	A	23.7.16	,,
3340	Pte.	Bulbeck, W. E.	D	23.7.16	,,
2178	Pte.	Castle, H. C.	D	23.7.16	,,
3591	Pte.	Cherrill, C. H.	B	23.7.16	,,
4700	Pte.	Clifton, H.	C	23.7.16	,,
2868	Pte.	Collett, S. T.	A	23.7.16	,,
3283	Pte.	Cox, O. B.	D	23.7.16	,,
5184	Pte.	Crook, J.	B	23.7.16	,,
4276	Pte.	Dean, A.	A	23.7.16	,,
5446	Pte.	Gosling, F.	B	23.7.16	,,
2445	Pte.	Green, F. W. A.	D	23.7.16	,,
2280	Pte.	Harris, J. F.	A	23.7.16	,,
4823	Pte.	Halsey, C.	A	23.7.16	,,
2120	Pte.	Higgins, H. V.	B	23.7.16	,,
2283	Pte.	Hudson, F. L.	B	23.7.16	,,
4788	Pte.	Ingram, W. J.	C	23.7.16	,,
4504	Pte.	Jenkins, F.	A	23.7.16	,,
2018	Pte.	Larkin, W.	D	23.7.16	,,
4033	Pte.	Lock, C.	B	23.7.16	,,
5212	Pte.	Osborne, G.	A	23.7.16	,,
1983	Pte.	Palmer, P. A.	A	23.7.16	,,
5110	Pte.	Parrott, A. B.	A	23.7.16	,,
2655	Pte.	Penson, A. R.	B	23.7.16	,,
2347	Pte.	Potter, M. D.	B	23.7.16	,,
4960	Pte.	Smith, M. H.	B	23.7.16	,,
5210	Pte.	Smith, N.	D	23.7.16	,,
3270	Pte.	Smith, R.	D	23.7.16	,,
3185	Pte.	Stroud, J.	D	23.7.16	,,
3018	Pte.	Styles, C. R.	A	23.7.16	,,
5138	Pte.	Sumner, R.	B	23.7.16	,,
3011	Pte.	Sirman, H.	A	23.7.16	,,
3685	Pte.	Tallett, A. S.	B	23.7.16	,,

1/4th OXF. & BUCKS LT. INFTY.

POZIERES—continued.

Regtl. No.	Rank.	Name.	Coy.		Date.	Place of Burial.
2669	Pte.	Tarrant, F.	B	Wounded	23.7.16	
				Died	14.8.16	Etaples
5004	Pte.	Taunt, G.	D		23.7.16	Pozieres
4722	Pte.	Thornton, F. W.	C	Wounded	23.7.16	
				Died	24.7.16	Warloy-Baillon
2916	Pte.	Turner, G.	B		23.7.16	Pozieres
4715	Pte.	Ward, H. G.	D		23.7.16	,,
5008	Pte.	Weston, H.	B		23.7.16	,,
2473	Pte.	Whiteley, A. L.	A		23.7.16	,,
5241	Pte.	Williams, W.	D		23.7.16	,,
4833	Pte.	Wright, W.	A		23.7.16	,,
1796	Bglr.	Treadwell, H.	B	Died	3.8.16	Agenville

POZIERES (Sky-Line Trench)—14.8.16.

Regtl. No.	Rank.	Name.	Coy.		Date.	Place of Burial.
	Capt.	Wayman, W. A.	A		14.8.16	Pozieres
	Lt.	Lakin, C.	B	Wounded	14.8.16	
				Died	21.8.16	Puchevillers
	2/Lt.	Hunter, L. W.	C		14.8.16	Pozieres
1990	Cpl.	Chatterton, J.	D	Wounded	14.8.16	
				Died	14.8.16	Puchevillers
1907	Cpl.	Hancox, W. R.	C		14.8.16	Pozieres
3566	L/C.	Ash, J.	C		14.8.16	,,
2494	L/C.	Blencowe, A.	C	Wounded	14.8.16	
				Died	16.8.16	Puchevillers
2315	L/C.	Hernon, T. W., M M.	D	Wounded	14.8.16	
				Died	24.8.16	Rouen
3257	L/C.	Hirons, C. F.	D	Wounded	14.8.16	
				Died	16.8.16	Aveluy
2519	L/C.	Humphries, R.	C.		14.8.16	Pozieres
3033	L/C.	Weston, F.	D		14.8.16	,,
2415	Pte.	Adams, A. S.	A		14.8.16	,,
6828	Pte.	Akers, A.	A		14.8.16	,,
6008	Pte.	Austin, J.	C		14.8.16	,,
4297	Pte.	Bonner, E. G.	D		14.8.16	,,
5222	Pte.	Bradfeld, W.	C		14.8.16	,,
1494	Pte.	Carpenter, H. G.	C		14.8.16	,,
4838	Pte.	Cleaver, R.	C		14.8.16	,,
4968	Pte.	Cobbett, F.	D		14.8.16	,,
3592	Pte.	Coventry, F.	B		14.8.16	,,

WAR RECORD OF THE

POZIERES—continued.

Regtl. No.	Rank.	Name.	Coy.		Date.	Place of Burial.
2568	Pte.	Cowley,. C. J.	A		14.8.16	Pozieres
4198	Pte.	Cull, H. A.	C		14.8.16	,,
4706	Pte.	Cummings, G.	D		14.8.16	,,
6125	Pte.	Essary, G.	A		14.8.16	,,
5047	Pte.	Evans, W.	C		14.8.16	,,
5834	Pte.	Freeman, H.	C		14.8.16	,,
4161	Pte.	Gable, W. J.	B		14.8.16	,,
5863	Pte.	Gomm. H.	C		14.8.16	,,
2782	Pte.	Hornblow, O.	D		14.8.16	,,
4818	Pte.	Hurst, C.	C		14.8.16	,,
3260	Pte.	James, A. S.	D		14.8.16	,,
3442	Pte.	Jones, G. F.	C		14.8.16	,,
5139	Pte.	King. A.	C		14.8.16	,,
3157	Pte.	Loveday, H. D.	C		14.8.16	,,
3342	Pte.	Lowe, J.	D		14.8.16	,,
5843	Pte.	Mace. F. E.	B		14.8.16	,,
3542	Pte.	Munday, W. E.	C		14.8.16	,,
4731	Pte.	Naish W.	D		14.8.16	,,
5845	Pte.	Newell. J.	D		14.8.16	,,
2595	Pte.	Nicholls. E.	C		14.8.16	,,
5062	Pte.	Pearce, E. H.	A		14.8.16	,,
5957	Pte.	Pease, W.	D		14.8.16	,,
6151	Pte.	Routley, H.	A		14.8.16	,,
5816	Pte.	Simmons, T.	C.	Wounded Died	14.8.16 18.8.16	Warloy-Baillon
3405	Pte.	Shurmer, T.	B		14.8.16	Pozieres
5026	Pte.	Thorne. F.	C		14.8.16	,,
5727	Pte.	Thorne, F. W.	A		14.8.16	,,
4771	Pte.	Turner, G.	C		14.8.16	,,
1774	Pte	Walton, J. H.	C		14.8.16	,,
3731	Pte.	White, A. J.	C		14.8.16	,,
3273	Pte.	Whiting, F. J.	C		14.8.16	,,
4210	Pte.	Woodley, F. A.	C		14.8.16	,,
5928	Pte.	Woodley, W. J.	C		14.8.16	,,

POZIERES (SKY-LINE TRENCH)—16.8.16—28.8.16.

5392	Pte.	Elliott, T. S.	A		16.8.16	Pozieres
5043	Pte.	Fuller, G. H.	B		16.8.16	,,
5979	Pte.	Gardner, T. H.	B	Wounded Died	16.8.16 22.8.16	Puchevillers

1/4th OXF. & BUCKS LT. INFTY.

POZIERS—continued.

Regtl No.	Rank.	Name.	Coy.		Date.	Place of Burial.
5838	Pte.	Gayton, W.	B		16.8.16	Pozieres
4717	Pte.	Pratley, W.	B		16.8.16	,,
4807	Pte.	Thomas, B.	A		16.8.16	,,
6153	Pte.	Thomas, W. H. C.	B		16.8.16	,,
6037	Pte.	Allen, J. H.	D		17.8.16	,,
1959	Sgt.	Cook, F.	D	Wounded	23.8.16	
				Died	26.8.16	Varennes
6802	Pte.	Millward, J.	D	Wounded	26.8.16	
				Died	1.9.16	Etaples
4865	Pte.	Payne, H.	D		23.8.16	Pozieres
5722	Pte.	Read, R.	D	Wounded	23.8.16	
				Died	24.8.16	Bouzincourt
3602	Pte.	Thornton, A. E.	C	Wounded	23.8.16	
				Died	28.8.16	Warloy-Baillon
5927	Pte.	Tolley, C.	B	Wounded	23.8.16	
				Died	26.8.16	Varennes
1635	L/C.	Birch, P. G.	D		24.8.16	Pozieres
1927	Pte.	Thompson, M.	D		24.8.16	,,
5985	Pte.	Hall, H.	D	Wounded	25.8.16	
				Died	26.8.16	Warloy-Baillon
6107	Pte.	Perkins, A.	A		25.8.16	Pozieres
3636	Pte.	Speaks, W. F.	A		26.8.16	,,
5966	Pte.	Tibble, A.	A		26.8.16	,,
2388	Pte.	Lainchbury, H. T. (Att'd Field Survey Coy)	B	Wounded Died	23.9.16 23.9.16	Mailly Maillet

LE SARS—2.11.16—12.12.16.

1723	L/C.	Whiteman, F.	B		5.11.16	Le Sars
20240	Pte.	Connop, A.	D	Wounded	5.11.16	
				Died	12.11.16	Rouen
5751	Pte.	Climpson, W. T.	B		5.11.16	Le Sars
6219	Pte.	Constable, P. C.	B	Wounded	5.11.16	
				Died	13.11.16	Bois-Guillaume
6350	Pte.	Green, A. J.	B		5.11.16	Le Sars
5654	Pte.	Keene, T. H.	B		5.11.16	,,
5800	Pte.	Larner, E.	B		5.11.16	,,
5692	Pte.	Loader, W.	B		5.11.16	,,

WAR RECORD OF THE

LE SARS—continued.

R gtl. No.	Rank	Name.	Coy.		Date.	Place of Burial.
6225	Pte.	Higgins, W.	B		7.11.16	Le Sars
4889	Pte.	Phipps, A.	A	Wounde	9.11.16	
				Died	24.11.16	Rouen
	Lt.	R. St. G. LAKE	A		17.11.16	Martinpuich
1893	Pte.	Eaton, R.	A		17.11.16	,,
3326	L/C.	Selcombe, A.	D		19.11.16	Le Sars
5178	Pte.	Gaunt, P.	D		19.11.16	,,
2090	Pte.	Harrison, G. H.	D	Wounded	19.11.16	
				Died	23.11.16	Dernancourt
6240	Pte.	Jacob, H.	C		19.11.16	Le Sars
5676	Pto.	Miles, S. E.	B		19.11.16	,,
5664	Pte.	Morris, C. H.	D		19.11.16	,,
5610	Pte.	Edgington, W.	C		20.11.16	,,
2233	Pte.	Field, M. A.	B		20.11.16	,,
20219	Pte.	Newland, W.	B	Wounded	20.11.16	
				Died	1.12.16	Dernancourt
23005	Pte.	Rowbotham, G. (Att'd 145 M.G.C.)			2.12.16	Le Sars
3440	Bglr.	Carter, W. E.	B	Wounded	5.12.16	
				Died	11.12.16	Dernancourt
5702	Pte.	Bolton, F. C.	C	Wounded	11.12.16	
				Died	13.12.16	Rouen
3653	Pte.	Hounslow, N.	C	Wounded	11.12.16	
				Died	11.12.16	Contalmaison
6190	Pte.	Legg, W. G.	C		11.12.16	Le Sars
6145	Pte.	White, W. G.	C	Wounded	11.12.16	
				Died	20.12.16	Boulogne
5034	Pte.	Schofield, E.	B	Died	20.12.16	Rouen

LA MAISONETTE, 7.2.17—17.3.17.

7543	Pte.	Eyols, E.	B	(Accdtly)	10.2.17	
				Died	12.2.17	Flaucourt
	2/Lt.	VOKES, B.	C		15.2.17	,,
235012	Pte.	Bampton, F. G.	D		15.2.17	,,
203417	Pte.	Wallen, W. H. G.	C	Wounded	26.2.17	
				Died	28.2.17	Bray
201106	Pte.	Gurl, A.	C		3.3.17	Flaucourt
201338	Pte.	Lomman, R.	B		12.3.17	,,
200726	L/C.	Taylor, S.	C		17.3.17	,,

1/4th OXF. & BUCKS LT. INFTY.

PERONNE—RONSSOY Advance, 20.3.17—5.4.17.

Regtl. No.	Rank.	Name	Coy.		Date.	Place of Burial.
200715	Pte.	Mapson, E. J.	D		25.3.17	Roisel
200505	L/C.	Wake, H. P.	B		26.3.17	Marquaix
203284	Pte.	Colmer, A. E.	B		26.3.17	,,
203046	Pte.	Fowler, W. J.	A		26.3.17	Roisel
203679	Pte.	Riley, W.	B	Wounded	26.3.17	
				Died	27.3.17	Bray
202250	Pte.	Summers, H.	A		26.3.17	Roisel
200524	L/C.	Waknell, L. G.	D	Wounded	31.3.17	
				Died	15.4.17	Rouen
203039	Pte.	Carthew, W. H.	B		4.4.17	Villers-Faucon
203607	Pte.	Chaplin, L.	D	Wounded	4.4.17	
				Died	4.4.17	Peronne
203207	Pte.	Ginger, A.	B	Wounded	4.4.17	Villers-Faucon
				Died	4.4.17	
203012	Pte.	Jeffrey, J. E.	B		4.4.17	,,
26355	Pte.	Richardson, J.	C	(Accdtly)	4.4.17	Ronssoy
203400	Pte.	Russell, W. E.	D	Died as Prisoner	4.4.17	Not known
200238	Cpl.	Burford, W. J.	D		5.4.17	Ronssoy
200659	Cpl.	Harris, H. T.	B		5.4.17	,,
201063	L/C.	Green, J. H.	A		5.4.17	,,
200154	L/C.	Shepherd, A.	C	Wounded	5.4.17	
				Died	11.4.17	Bray
203275	Pte.	Busby, P.	C		5.4.17	Ronssoy
202409	Pte.	Doble, J.	C		5.4.17	,,
202534	Pte.	Flitt, J. T.	A		5.4.17	,,
202522	Pte.	Ridd, S.	C		5.4.17	,,
200451	Pte.	Rowlands, G. F.	B		5.4.17	,,
203692	Pte.	Sammons, M. H.	C		5.4.17	,,
202419	Pte.	Harris, J.	B	Wounded	5.4.17	
				Died	6.4.17	Bray

GILLEMONT FARM, 19.4.17.

	2/Lt.	Dinwoodie, D. W. (8th Scottish R.)	D		19.4.17	Ronssoy
201365	Sgt.	French, A.	D		19.4.17	,,
200467	Sgt.	Herbert, W. G.	D		19.4.17	,,
203936	Cpl.	Selwyn, R.	A	Wounded	19.4.17	
				Died	25.4.17	Rouen

WAR RECORD OF THE

GILLEMONT FARM—continued.

Regtl. No.	Rank	Name	Coy.		Date.	Place of Burial.
235011	L/C.	Godfrey, H. A.	D	Wounded	19.4.17	
				Died	21.4.17	Peronne
202357	L/C.	Smith, D.	D		19.4.17	
202153	Pte.	Aries, G. H.	D	Wounded	19.4.17	
				Died as Prisoner	20.4.17	Not known
203895	Pte.	Avenall, C.	D		19.4.17	Ronssoy
203353	Pte	Bailey, A.	D	Wounded	19.4.17	
				Died	20.4.17	Templeux-la-Fosse
202537	Pte.	Bowler, A.	D		19.4.17	Ronssoy
203290	Pte.	Dorsett, F. J.	D		19.4.17	,,
203612	Pte.	Green, T. G.	D		19.4.17	,,
26705	Pte.	Henson, G.	D		19.4.17	,,
201330	Pte.	Hill, H. G.	A		19.4.17	,,
202411	Pte.	Hooper, R. F.	D		19.4.17	,,
200398	Pte.	Maidment, C.	D		19.4.17	,,
17537	Pte.	Maker, H. J.	D	Wounded	19.4.17	
				Died	20.4.17	Peronne
200930	Pte.	May, E. A.	D		19.4.17	Ronssoy
200266	Pte.	Yates, T. W.	D		19.4.17	,,
22902	L/C.	Wilsdon, H. (Att'd 145 M.G.C.)		Wounded	26.4.17	
				Died	29.4.17	La Chapellotte
200475	Pte.	Green, J. A.		Died	7.5.17	Rouen

HERMIES AND DEMICOURT, 14.5.17—2.7.17.

201253	Sgt.	Drewitt, A.	C		21.5.17	Hermies
200385	L/C.	Kitchen, E. J.	B		21.5.17	,,
203371	Pte.	Hanks, E.	C		21.5.17	,,
203552	Pte.	Wallis, G. A.	A	Wounded	21.5.17	
				Died as Prisoner	18.9.17	Stettin, Germany
204398	Pte.	Brown, F. V.	D		25.5.17	Hermies
201927	Pte.	Laurence, F.	B		31.5.17	Demicourt
200582	Cpl.	Allington, J. (Att'd 145 T.M. Bty.)			8.6.17	Hermies
200101	Pte.	Smith, J. T.	B	Wounded	24.6.17	
				Died	26.6.17	Grevillers.

1/4th OXF. & BUCKS LT. INFTY. 65

YPRES, 31.7.17.

Regtl. No.	Rank.	Name.	Coy		Date.	Place of Burial.
202217	Pte.	Allen, H. (Att'd 145 M.G.C.)	A	Wounded Died	31.7.17 31.7.17	Poperinghe
203317	Pte.	Maccaboo, E. J. (Att'd 145 M.G.C.)	B		31.7.17	S. Julien
203323	Pte.	Pidwell, P. (Att'd 145 M.G.C.)	C		31.7.17	,,

YPRES, 5.8.17—8.8.17.

Regtl. No.	Rank.	Name.	Coy		Date.	Place of Burial.
	2/Lt.	WHITE, R. H., M.C. (25th London Regt. 56th. Div. Cyc. Coy.)			5.8.17	,,
	2/Lt.	GIBSON, H. E.			7.8.17	,,
200024	R.S.M.	Lane, W. R.	A		5.8.17	,,
200513	Sgt.	Butt, H.	C	Wounded Died	7.8.17 7.8.17	Proven
203884	Sgt.	Ross, A.	D		8.8.17	S. Julien
200490	Cpl.	Bannard, P.	C		7.8.17	,,
200804	Cpl.	Christian, A. S.	D	Wounded Died	8.8.17 8.8.17	Elverdinghe
8094	Cpl.	Reynolds, F. B.	D		5.8.17	S Julien
201845	Cpl.	Sammons, R. E.	C		7.8.17	,,
201190	L/C.	Burton, W. E.	D		8.8.17	,,
10491	L/C.	Gardner, R. H.	C		7.8.17	,,
203918	L/C.	Hockey, C. E.	B		8.8.17	Wieltje
203396	L/C.	Jackman, R. C.	D		8.8.17	S. Julien
200698	Bglr.	Tucker, L. J.	A	Wounded Died	8.8.17 24.8.17	Boulogne
202173	Pte.	Birch, W.	A	Wounded Died	7.8.17 15.8.17	Etaples
203045	Pte.	Elkington, W.	A		5.8.17	S. Julien
200439	Pte.	Fowler, E. J.	B		8.8.17	Wieltje
33488	Pte.	Grant, W. J.	A		5.8.17	S. Julien
201746	Pte.	Green, C.	C	Wounded Died	7.8.17 7.8.17	Proven
201875	Pte.	Harper, E.	D		8.8.17	S. Julien
24399	Pte.	Hillsdon, H.	C		7.8.17	,,
202603	Pte.	Hunt, W. H.	D		8.8.17	,,
201602	Pte.	Jacobs, F.	A		7.8.17	,,
266312	Pte.	Jackson, A. T.	C		7.8.17	,,

E

WAR RECORD OF THE

YPRES—continued.

Regtl. No.	Rank.	Name.	Coy.		Date.	Place of Burial.
203892	Pte.	Kemp, A.	C	Wounded	7.8.17	
				Died	17.8.17	Etaples
203390	Pte.	Oates, G.	D	Wounded	5.8.17	
				Died	13.8.17	Vlamertinghe
28420	Pte.	Piddock, W.	B	Wounded	8.8.17	
				Died	9.8.17	Proven
201605	Pte.	Reynolds, L. P.	C		7.8.17	S. Julien
32559	Pte.	Richardson, R.	C		8.8.17	,,
202404	Pte.	Townsend, H.	B		8.8.17	Wieltje
203663	Pte.	Watson, E.	A		7.8.17	S. Julien
202429	Pte.	Withers, C.	A		6.8.17	,,

YPRES, 16.8.17.

Regtl. No.	Rank.	Name.	Coy.		Date.	Place of Burial.
	2/Lt.	BOWMAN, C. H.	A		16.8.17	S. Julien
	2/Lt.	JEFFERSON, H.	C		16.8.17	,,
	2/Lt.	JONES, F. E., M.C.	D		16.8.17	,,
	2/Lt.	SALMON, A. F.	C		16.8.17	,,
	2/Lt.	WOTHERSPOON, A. S.	B		16.8.17	,,
200627	Sgt.	Burden, G. H.	A		16.8.17	,,
200563	Sgt.	Singleton, A. J.	C		16.8.17	
266122	L/Sgt.	Norwood, A.	B		16.8.17	
203262	L/Sgt.	Wright, J. R.	A		16.8.17	,,
203878	Cpl.	Brown, E. A.	C		16.8.17	,,
200145	Cpl.	Giles, A. E.	C		16.8.17	,,
29243	Cpl.	Hubbard, J. T.	D		16.8.17	,,
200173	Cpl.	King, L.	C		16.8.17	,,
200005	Cpl.	Mold, J. H.	C		16.9.17	,,
200539	Cpl.	Robinson, F.	C		16.8.17	,,
200529	L/C.	Adams, F. J.	A		16.8.17	,,
200348	L/C.	Allen, W.	C		16.8.17	,,
200421	L/C.	Andrews, R.	B		16.8.17	,,
11588	L/C.	Benfield, A. F.	D		16.8.17	,,
22969	L/C.	Bird, S.	D		16.8.17	,,
200527	L/C.	Burden, R. G.	A	Wounded	16.8.17	
				Died	18.8.17	Elverdinghe
202489	L/C.	Gliddon, P. J.	B		16.8.17	S. Julien
200183	L/C.	Hieatt, S. G.	C		16.8.17	,,
201704	L/C.	Hutson, S.	A		17.8.17	,,
201567	L/C.	Messenger, P.	D		16.8.17	,,
201600	L/C.	Partlett, J. F.	B		16.8.17	,,
201427	L/C.	Radbone, J.	D		16.8.17	,,

1/4th OXF. & BUCKS LT. INFTY.

YPRES—continued.

Regtl. No.	Rank.	Name	Coy.		Date.	Place of Burial.
202515	L/C.	Radford, W. J.	C		16.8.17	S. Julien
11830	L/C.	Wilkinson, B. H.	A		16.8.17	,,
200654	Bglr.	Cudd, T.	A	Wounded Died	17.8.17 18.8.17	Elverdinghe
201599	Bglr.	Howe, W.	C		16.8.17	S. Julien
15046	Pte.	Asplay, J.	C		16.8.17	,,
203354	Pte.	Baker, W.	A		16.8.17	,,
200447	Pte.	Blencowe, A.	C	Wounded Died	16.8.17 4.9.17	Elverdinghe
200981	Pte.	Compton, W. J.	D		16.8.17	S. Julien
235007	Pte.	Cowley, A.	D		16.8.17	,,
202526	Pte.	Dingle, L.	C		16.8.17	,,
203684	Pte.	Eadle, J.	A		16.8.17	,,
203370	Pte.	Grain, H. G.	C	Wounded Died	16.8.17 27.8.17	Elverdinghe
16335	Pte.	Green, G. E.	D		16.8.17	S. Julien
202345	Pte.	Hathaway, W. G.	B		16.8.17	,,
203374	Pte.	Hathaway, F. A	A		16.8.17	,,
201432	Pte.	Holloway, C.	D		16.8.17	,,
203303	Pte.	Howkins, J.	B		16.8.17	,,
13998	Pte.	Hunt, E. W.	D		16.8.17	,,
201343	Pte.	Hutchins, F.	A		16.8.17	,,
202740	Pte.	James, F. A.	D		16.8.17	,,
200788	Pte.	Jelfs, E. C.	D		16.8.17	,,
200330	Pte.	Keene, J.	A		16.8.17	,,
202248	Pte.	Kirby, A. J.	A		16.8.17	,,
203896	Pte.	Larkins, C. W.	D		16.8.17	,,
203916	Pte.	Life, J.	A		16.8.17	,,
202347	Pte.	Louch, J.	A		16.8.17	,,
15930	Pte.	Lyford, E.	C		16.8.17	,,
203382	Pte	May, A. W.	D		16.8.17	,,
202412	Pte.	Mock, G.	D	Wounded Died	16.8.17 16.8.17	Vlamertinghe
203321	Pte.	Murray, D. A.	A		17.8.17	S. Julien
32917	Pte.	Nash, A.	D		16.8.17	,,
203389	Pte.	Neale, E. J.	B		16.8.17	,,
203625	Pte.	Norgrove, S. J.	B		16.8.17	,,
201600	Pte.	Nutt, H.	C		16.8.17	,,
27970	Pte.	Orchard, F.	A		17.8.17	,,
33085	Pte.	Partingdon, A. J.	C		16.8.17	,,
202353	Pte.	Pike, E. H.	A		16.8.17	,,

WAR RECORD OF THE

YPRES—continued.

Regtl. No.	Rank.	Name.	Coy.		Date.	Place of Burial.
23659	Pte.	Powell, P.	A	Wounded	17.8.17	
				Died	18.8.17	Elverdinghe
203162	Pte.	Richard, G.	D		16.8.17	S. Julien
203340	Pte.	Serman, A. W.	A		16.8.17	,,
201616	Pte.	Simson, G.	C		16.8.17	,,
203338	Pte.	Smith, H.	D		16.8.17	,,
201667	Pte.	Stannard, W.	B		16.8.17	,,
267518	Pte.	Swindle, V. V.	B		16.8.17	,,
203694	Pte.	Turner, H. E.	C		16.8.17	,,
201674	Pte.	Webb, A.	D		16.8.17	,,
201234	Pte.	White, J.	C		16.8.17	,,
200167	Pte.	Winterbourne, W.	B	Wounded	16.8.17	
				Died	20.8.17	Elverdinghe
33321	Pte.	Woodruff, W. A.	C		16.8.17	S.Julien
203696	Pte.	Woodwards, A.	C		16.8.17	,,
203691	Pte.	Woolhead, W. (Att'd 145 T.M.B.)	B		16.8.17	,,

YPRES, 27.8.17.

203567	Cpl.	Collier, F. G.	C		27.8.17	,,
235002	L/C.	Quick, H.	D		28.8.17	,,
202131	Bglr.	Lydford, C.	B		27.8.17	,,
265709	Pte.	Bonham, A. T.	A		27.8.17	,,
28544	Pte.	Cox, J. J.	A	Wounded	27.8.17	
				Died	1.9.17	Proven
202223	Pte.	Dean, H.	A		27.8.17	S. Julien
203573	Pte.	Fielden, H. T.	A	Wounded	27.8.17	
				Died	27.8.17	,,
202488	Pte.	Palmer, P.	C		27.8.17	,,
201208	Pte.	Shayler, F. H.	A		27.8.17	,,
203600	Pte.	Webb, A. J.	A		27.8.17	,,

YPRES, 27.9.17—10.10.17.

	Capt.	Birt, L. W.		Wounded	27.9.17	
				Died	3.10.17	Proven
200799	L/C.	Bradfield, B. W.	D	Wounded	28.9.17	,,
				Died	3.10.17	
201772	Pte.	Alder, H.	C		28.9.17	S. Julien
26150	Pte.	Bishop, F.	C		30.9.17	,,
18091	Pte.	Evans, H.	A		2.10.17	,,

1/4th OXF. & BUCKS LT. INFTY.

YPRES – continued.

Regtl. No.	Rank	Name.	Coy.		Date.	Place of Burial
20250	Pte.	Good, A. E.	B		30.9.17	S. Julien
25537	Pte.	Hooper, S.	C		30.9.17	,,
200073	Pte.	Jeffrey, H.	A		27.9.17	,,
19385	Pte.	King, H. G.	A		2.10.17	,,
28870	Pte.	Loach, W.	A	Wounded Died	2.10.17 7.10.17	Etaples
29240	Pte.	Moore, A.	D		2.10.17	S. Julien
26264	Pte.	Mucklow, J.	C		30.9.17	,,
28561	Pte.	Turner, A.	D		28.9.17	,,
26147	Pte.	Stokes, H.	C	(Accdtly)	8.10.17	,,
201847	L/C.	Binham, H. (Att d 145 M.G.C.)	A	Wounded Died	10.10.17 12.10.17	Provon
202474	Pte.	Rowe, W. H. (Att d 145 M.G.C.)	C		10.10.17	S. Julien

VIMY, 2.11.17—10.11.17.

201553	Pte.	Bowerman, A.	B		4.11.17	Thelus
201821	Pte.	Preston, J.	B		4.11.17	,,
203314	Pte.	Lisemore, A.	B		5.11.17	,,
203986	Pte.	Sharratt, B. (Att'd 185 Tunn. Coy.)	B		8.11.17	,,
23047	Pte.	Mitton, C. W.	C	Died	19.11.17	Aubigny

ITALY, 28.11.17—14.6.18.

20251	Pte.	Hope, G. H.	C	Died	12.12.17	Mantova
26339	Pte.	Miles, H. W. H.	B	Died	31.1.18	Cremona
202398	Pte.	Owens, H. J.	B		15.5.18	Granezza
202458	Cpl.	Elliman, W. H.	A		19.5.18	Barenthal

AUSTRIAN OFFENSIVE, 15.6.18.

	Rank	Name	Coy.		Date	Place
	Capt.	ALLAN, A., M.C.	C	Wounded Died	15.6.18 17.6.18	Montecchio
	Capt.	BUXTON, R. P.	D		15.6.18	Boscon
	Lt.	GARLICK, V.	B		15.6.18	,,
	2/Lt.	BUTTERY, R. A.	C		15.6.18	,,
	2/Lt.	LUCK, N. A. (R.W. Kents).	D		15.6.18	,,
	2/Lt.	MOORE, T.	A.		15.6.18	,,
200260	Sgt.	Grimsley, J. H.	B		15.6.18	,,

WAR RECORD OF THE

AUSTRIAN OFFENSIVE—continued.

Regtl. No.	Rank.	Name.	Coy.		Date.	Place of Burial.
201141	Sgt.	Harris, W. C.	A		15.6.18	Boscon
200224	L/Sgt.	Sargood, R.	C		15.6.18	,,
201555	L/Sgt.	Waterman, G. T., M.M.	B	Wounded	15.6.18	
				Died	22.6.18	Montecchio
200609	Cpl.	Marrison. C.	C		15.6.18	Boscon
203358	L/C.	Clinkard, K. C.	B		15.6.18	,,
200497	L/C.	Gash, E.	C		15.6.18	,,
200677	L/C.	Gray, C. C.	B	Wounded		
				Died	24.6.18	Montecchio
11201	L/C.	Knight, J.	A		15.6.18	Boscon
200649	L/C.	Mace, A. G.	B		15.6.18	,,
203331	L/C.	Robson, E. W.	B		15.6.18	,,
202987	L/C.	Walker, W. F.	B		15.6.18	,,
29245	Pte.	Bagley, H. G.	B		15.6.18	,,
26165	Pte.	Brayford, E. S.	D		15.6.18	,,
203357	Pte.	Bumpass, K.	A		15.6.18	,,
201759	Pte.	Callaghan, M.	A		15.6.18	,,
203904	Pte.	Cooper, G.	A		15.6.18	,,
12025	Pte.	Cooper, J.	B		15.6.18	,,
200312	Pte.	Cox, W. A.	B		15.6.18	,,
200639	Pte.	Day, T.	D		15.6.18	,,
11386	Pte.	Derricott, H.	C		15.6.18	,,
202102	Pte.	Faulkener, H. G.	B		15.6.18	,,
21318	Pte.	Golby, E.	C		15.6.18	,,
203097	Pte.	Halls, W.	A		15.6.18	,,
202208	Pte.	Hands, J.	C		15.6.18	,,
202602	Pte.	Holland, J.	D	Wounded	15.6.18	
				Died	20.6.18	Montecchio
201737	Pte.	Horwood, A. V.	D		15.6.18	Boscon
203577	Pte.	Hewish, E. C.	B.		15.6.18	,,
266613	Pte.	Kent, A. T.	B		15.6.18	,,
203313	Pte.	Lane, A. F.	B		15.6.18	,,
203217	Pte.	Launchbury, A.	B		15.6.18	,,
201697	Pte.	Madden, T.	D	Wounded	15.6.18	
				Died	16.6.18	Montecchio
201756	Pte.	Mitchell, G.	B	Wounded	15.6.18	
				Died	19.6.18	,,
200370	Pte.	Morris, G.	D	Wounded	15.6.18	
				Died	17.6.18	,,
204475	Pte.	Naylor, P.	C	Wounded	15.6.18	
				Died	18.6.18	Genoa

1/4th OXF. & BUCKS LT. INFTY.

AUSTRIAN OFFENSIVE—continued.

Regtl. No.	Rank.	Name.	Coy.		Date.	Place of Burial.
206416	Pte.	Parker, B.	B		15.6.18	Boscon
7848	Pte.	Pearce, E.	A		15.6.18	,,
266437	Pte.	Priest, W.	B		15.6.18	,,
203330	Pte.	Robbins, W. R.	A		15.6.18	,,
9663	Pte.	Robinson, W. H.	B		15.6.18	,,
202314	Pte.	Shillingford, A.	A		15.6.18	,,
200618	Pte.	Taylor, H. A.	A		15.6.18	,,
204394	Pte.	Walford, A.	B		15.8.18	,,
28996	Pte.	Walton, E.	C		15.6.18	,,
29619	Pte.	Walton, E. A.	A		15.6.18	,,
200542	Pte.	Watson, G. A.	C		15.6.18	,,
203597	Pte.	Woodley, T. J.	A		15.6.18	,,
201744	Pte.	Woodward, G.	A	Wounded	15.6.18	
				Died	22.6.18	Montecchio

ITALY, 20.7.18—9.9.18.

14085	Pte.	Mobbs, G. F.	B	Died	29.6.18	Cavaletto
202285	Pte.	Buchanan, C.	B	Died	27.7.18	Sangatte
		(Att'd 271 Rail. Lab. Coy, R.E.)				
200792	Cpl.	Bateman, P.	A	Wounded	8.8.18	
				Died	8.8.18	Granezza
23642	Pte.	Butler, S.	A	Wounded	8.8.18	
				Died	10.8.18	Montecchio

RAID ON SEC, 10.9.18.

200840	Cpl.	Rollings, W. G.	B	Wounded	10.9.18	
				Died	23.9.18	Cavaletto
23085	L/C.	Taylor, E. F.	C	Wounded	10.9.18	
				Died	10.9.18	,,
202422	Pte.	Kingdom, F.	C	Wounded	10.9.18	
				Died	10.9.18	Barenthal
201673	Pte.	Nash, F. W.	B		10.9.18	,,

ITALY, 11.9.18—24.3.19.

200719	L/C.	Evans, W.	D		11.10.18	Granezza
14521	Sgt.	Isham, F. L.	C	Died	20.10.18	Brackley England
46943	Pte.	Mayall, S. H.	B	Died	24.10.18	Bordighera

SUMMARY OF HONOURS & AWARDS.

BREVET MAJOR	1
BAR TO D.S.O.	1
D.S.O.	5
BAR TO M.C.	1
M.C.	28
D.C.M.	11
BAR TO M.M.	3
M.M.	76
M.S.M.	11
ITALIAN SILVER MEDAL FOR VALOUR	4
ITALIAN BRONZE MEDAL FOR VALOUR	2
ITALIAN CROCE DI GUERRA	9
BELGIAN CROIX DE GUERRE	1
MENTIONS IN DESPATCHES	55
TOTAL	208

1/4th OXF. & BUCKS LT. INFTY. 75

HONOURS AND AWARDS
To OFFICERS Serving with the 48th Division.

Name.	Action.	Date of London Gazette.
BREVET MAJOR.		
Lt.-Col. A. J. N. Bartlett		1.1.17
BAR TO D.S.O.		
Lt.-Col. A. J. N. Bartlett, D.S.O.	Asiago (Austrian Attack)	24.9.18
D.S.O.		
Major R. L. Ovey (attd. 145 Bde. Bomb School)	Hebuterne	14.1.16
Major J. O. Summerhayes (R.A.M.C.)	Pozieres (Sickle Trench)	26.9.16
Lt.-Col. A. J. N. Bartlett	Ypres	1.1.18
Major A. B. Lloyd-Baker (1st Bucks)	,,	,,
Major P. Pickford, M.C.	Asiago (Austrian Attack)	24.9.18
BAR TO M.C.		
Lt. H. Miles, M.C.	Ave (Raid)	16.8.18
M.C.		
Capt. B. Long (attd. M.G.C.)	Ploegsteert	14.1.16
Capt. P. Pickford	,,	,,
Capt. G. K. Rose	,,	,,
Major J. J. Conybeare	Hebuterne	3.6.16
*2/Lt. F. E. Jones	Pozieres (Sickle Trench)	22.9.16
The Rev. K. Jackson (C.F.)	,,	,,
2/Lt. C. E. R. Sherrington	Pozieres (Sky-Line Trench)	26.9.16
Capt. F. B. Jones	Somme	1.1.17
Capt. E. E. Bridges	,,	,,
Capt. J. C. Coombes (attd. T.M.B.)	,,	,,
*2/Lt. R. H. White (25th London Regt.)	Peronne (Advance)	11.5.17
Capt. G. H. Greenwell	,,	,,

WAR RECORD OF THE

M.C.—continued.

Name.	Action.	Date of London Gazette.
*2/Lt. A. Allan	ROISEL (ADVANCE)	26.5.17
Lt. T. R. Fortescue	GILLEMONT FARM	18.6.17
2/Lt. H. Miles	YPRES	26.11.17
Capt. A. K. Gibson	ITALY	3.6.18
Lt. J. M. Constable	ASIAGO (AUSTRIAN ATTACK)	24.9.18
2/Lt. W. R. Vince	,,	,,
Capt. J. E. Boyle	SEC (RAID)	2.12.18
Capt. W. H. Enoch	,,	,,
2/Lt. W. R. B. Brooks	,,	,,
2/Lt. J. F. Wright	,,	,,
Capt. J. E. Mackay	ASIAGO	1.1.19
2/Lt. J. T. Foster	AUSTRIA (ADVANCE)	2.4.19
R.S.M. H. E. Buckingham	,,	,,
Lt. J. C. B. Gamlen (attd. 48 Div. H.Q.)	ITALY	2.6.19
Capt. J. B. Matthews (R.A.M.C.)	,,	,,
2/Lt. E. E. Howell	,,	,,

ITALIAN SILVER MEDAL FOR VALOUR.

Capt. J. E. Mackay	ASIAGO	29.11.18
Major P. Pickford, D.S.O., M.C.	SEC (RAID)	11.3.19
Capt. W. P. Powell	,,	,,

ITALIAN BRONZE MEDAL FOR VALOUR.

2/Lt. J. F. Wright, M.C.	SEC (RAID)	11.3.19

ITALIAN CROCE DI GUERRA.

Lt.-Col. A. J. N. Bartlett, D.S.O.	AUSTRIA (ADVANCE)	17.5.19
Capt. W. H. Enoch, M.C.	,,	,,
Capt. B. Long. (attd. M.G.C.)	,,	,,
2/Lt. G. E. Webster	,,	,,

MENTIONED IN DESPATCHES.

Name.	Date.
Major J. A. Ballard	1.1.16
Major R. L. Ovey	,,
Capt. B. Long (attd. M.G.C.)	,,
Capt. P. Pickford	,,
Capt. G. K. Rose	,,
Capt. F. B. Jones	30.4.16

1/4th OXF. & BUCKS LT. INFTY.

MENTIONED IN DESPATCHES—continued.

Name.	Date.
Lt.-Col. A. J. N. Bartlett	4.1.17
Major and Q.M. A. A. Bridgewater	,,
Major B. Long, M.C. (attd. M.G.C.)	,,
Lt. A. K. Gibson	25.5.17
Lt.-Col. A. J. N. Bartlett	21.12.17
Major A. B. Lloyd Baker (1st Bucks)	,,
Lt. W. P. Powell	,,
2/Lt. A. E. Crew	,,
Lt. W. H. Enoch	,,
Major A. B. Lloyd Baker (1st Bucks)	30.5.18
Capt. J. C. Coombes, M.C. (attd. T.M.B.)	,,
Lt. J. M. Constable	,,
Lt. J. E. Mackay	,,
R.S.M. H. E. Buckingham	,,
Lt.-Col. A. J. N. Bartlett, D.S.O.	6.1.19
2/Lt. J. T. Foster	,,
2/Lt. E. E. Howell	,,
Major B. Long, M.C. (attd. M.G.C.)	,,
Major P. Pickford, D.S.O., M.C.	,,
Rev. J. Henderson (C.F.)	,,
Capt. J. B. Matthews (R.A.M.C.)	,,
2/Lt. C. E. Moon.	3.6.19
Capt. and Q.M. J. T. Corrie (Manchester Regt.)	,,

1/4th OXF. & BUCKS LT. INFTY. 79

HONOURS AND AWARDS
To N.C.O.s & MEN Serving with the 48th Division.

D.C.M.

No.	Name.	Coy.	Action.	Date of London Gazette.
*2207	Sgt. J. S. C. King	B	PLOEGSTEERT	14.1.16
2470	Pte. L. H. Senior	C	,,	,,
1440	Sgt. H. A. Clark	D	POZIERES (SICKLE TRENCH)	22.9.16
1362	Sgt. L. Crowe	C	POZIERES (SKY-LINE TRENCH)	26.9.16
2249	Cpl. E. A. Mazey	C	,,	,,
200100	C.S.M. W. J. Coggins	C	AVE (RAID)	16.8.18
18430	Cpl. J. H. Stratford	A	ASIAGO (AUSTRIAN ATTACK)	30.10.18
8672	L/C. F. S. Spicer	B	,,	,,
201572	Cpl. L. A. Cripps (attd. T.M.B.)		,,	,,
200410	Cpl. F. R. Crombleholme	C	SEC (RAID)	11.3.19
200728	L/Sgt. A. C. Caiger (attd. 145 Bde. H.Q.)			

BAR TO M.M.

201785	Sgt. W. N. Hobbs, M.M	B	YPRES	2.11.17
200229	Sgt. A. W. Lemmings, M.M.	B	SEC (RAID)	24.1.19
13294	Pte. G. Daniells, M.M.	A	,,	,,

M.M.

178	Sgt. L. H. Griffin	H.Q.	HEBUTERNE	3.6.16
2695	Sgt. J. H. Mattinson	C	,,	,,
1752	Sgt. H. Collier (attd. M.G.C.)		HEBUTERNE	10.11.16
1794	Sgt. B. W. Fairman	A	,,	,,
*2488	Sgt. F. Newman	C	,,	,,
2292	Sgt. J. Woolnough	C	,,	,,
1671	Sgt. A. H. Wooton	D	,,	,,
2346	Cpl. G. W. Adkins (attd. T.M.B.)		,,	,,
1579	L/C. A. Admans	B	,,	,,
1938	L/C. G. Ashplant	A	,,	,,
201089	L/C. A. T. Turner	D	,,	,,

WAR RECORD OF THE

M.M. continued.

No.	Name.	Coy.	Action.	Date of London Gazette.
1427	Bandsman T. Carter	B	,,	10.11.16
2674	Pte. J. H. Abraham (attd. 145 Bde Bomb School)		,,	
*1654	C.S.M. J. T. Peet	D	HEBUTERNE	19.2.17
*1776	Sgt. T. P. Barlow	D	,,	,,
201233	L/C. T. Ward	A	POZIERES	21.9.16
3530	Sgt. A. Enstone	A	SOMME	21.10.16
*1700	Cpl. R. W. Stevens	B	,,	,,
1585	L/C. B. W. Harbod	C	,,	,,
*2315	L/C. T. W. Hermon	D	,,	,,
3057	Pte. L. W. Hawkins	H.Q.	,,	,,
4262	Pte. A. Margetts	B	,,	,,
3616	Pte. F. G. Millin	B	,,	,,
*3584	Pte. E. W. Thomas	C	,,	,,
200335	Pte. T. H. Smith	H.Q.	PERONNE	26.4.17
203615	Pte. J. E. Godwin	H.Q.	,,	,,
200735	Sgt. W. H. Mudge	B	ROISEL-RONSSOY	26.5.17
201040	L/Sgt. A. C. H. Wiggins	B	,,	,,
200793	L/C. B. Batts	B	,,	,,
201785	L/C. W. N. Hobbs	B	,,	,,
200399	L/C. J. Upstone	B	,,	,,
200462	L/C. F. G. Wilson	C	,,	,,
200482	Pte. J. T. White	C	,,	,,
200631	Sgt. H. A. Harris	D	GILLEMONT FARM	18.6.17
201116	Cpl. R. J. Collier	D	,,	,,
200602	Cpl. G. Kimberley	D	,,	,,
200774	L/C. G. J. Leeds	D	,,	,,
201472	Pte. E. Ayres	D	,,	,,
201129	Pte. R. G. Chamings	D	,,	,,
203383	Pte. A. W. May		,,	,,
200072	Sgt. F. Haley	B	YPRES	2.11.17
200077	L/C. C. C. Gray	H.Q.	,,	,,
201728	Pte. H. J. Finch	B	,,	,,
200749	Pte. H. S. Pearce	A	,,	,,
200003	C.Q.M.S. W. J. Liebermann	D	ASIAGO (AUSTRIAN ATTACK)	21.10.18
202990	Sgt. A. Disbury	C	,,	,,
200229	Sgt. A. W. Lemmings	B	,,	,,
*203559	Sgt. G. T. Waterman	B	,,	,,
200790	L/C. F. H. Atkins	D	,,	,,
203418	L/C. S. W. Wilks	B	,,	,,
202164	L/C. E. H. Wyatt	A	,,	,,

1/4th OXF. & BUCKS LT. INFTY.

M.M.—continued.

No.	Name.	Coy.	Action.	Date of London Gazette.
266908	Pte. F. A. Allen	D	,,	,,
13294	Pte. G. Daniells	A	,,	,,
9349	Pte. H. Richards	A	,,	,,
29423	Pte. H. H. Ryland	C	,,	,,
201858	Sgt. H. A. Burden	A	Sec (Raid)	24.1.19
201228	Sgt. A. G. Cooper	B	,,	,,
201552	Sgt. G. Harris	B	,,	,,
200157	Sgt. T. F. Wynne	C	,,	,,
200286	Cpl. W. G. Clements	A	,,	,,
203584	Cpl. E. T. Ollsen	C	,,	,,
201619	Cpl. E. Rixon	B	,,	,,
200507	L/C. J. T. Dyer	A	,,	,,
200519	L/C. H. C. Harris	A	,,	,,
26670	Bglr. H. W. Bennett	C	,,	,,
10456	Pte. A. Hall	C	,,	,,
33015	Pte. F. Price	A	,,	,,
200745	Pte. H. Saunders	B	,,	,,
265515	C.S.M. T. Avery	B	Austria (Advance)	29.3.19
200274	Sgt. A. S. Garrett	H.Q.	,,	,,
203380	Sgt. L. D. Howells	H.Q.	,,	,,
200362	Sgt. H. J. Howse	A	,,	,,
200022	Cpl. G. T. Douglas	H.Q.	,,	,,
203908	L/C. J. S. Farr	H.Q.	,,	,,
200602	L/C. A. C. Tomlin	D	,,	,,
11346	Pte. A. Hudson	C	,,	,,

M.S.M.

No.	Name.	Coy.	Date.
200400	Sgt. H. F. Jeynes	H.Q.	3.6.18
200026	R.Q.M.S. J. Burford	H.Q.	,,
200251	C.Q.M.S. H. J. Harmsworth	C	1.1.19
200136	Sgt. A. G. E. Russell	H.Q.	,,
201929	Cpl. R. Sansome (attd. T.M.B.)		,,
200505	L/C. W. H. Lloyd (attd. 145 Bde H.Q.)		,,
200695	Sgt. L. S. Stratford	..	,,
200009	C.Q.M.S. W. J. Liebermann, M.M.	H.Q.	3.6.19
200176	Sgt. O. Frewin	H.Q.	,,
200662	Cpl. W. H. Goddard	H.Q.	,,

ITALIAN SILVER MEDAL FOR VALOUR.

No.	Name.	Coy.	Action.	Date.
18430	Cpl. J. H. Stratford. D.C.M.	A	Asiago (Austrian Attack)	29.11.18

F

ITALIAN BRONZE MEDAL FOR VALOUR.

No.	Name.	Coy.	Action.	Date of London Gazette.
200410	Cpl. F. R. Crombleholme, D.C.M.	C	Sec (Raid)	11.3.19

ITALIAN CROCE DI GUERRA.

203397	Cpl. W. R. Price	H.Q.	Asiago	29.11.18
210619	Cpl. E. Rixon, M.M.	B	Sec (Raid)	11.3.19
201233	Cpl. T. Ward, M.M.	A	,,	,,
201259	L/C. E. H. Luckett	B	,,	,,
203380	Sgt. L. D. Howells, M.M.	H.Q.	Austria (Advance)	17.5.19
203397	Pte. C Jeffs (attd. T.M.B.)		,,	,,

BELGIAN CROIX DE GUERRE.

No.	Name.	Coy.	Date.
200262	L/C. P. Millin	B	12.7.18

LONG SERVICE AND GOOD CONDUCT.

6012	R.S.M. H. E. Buckingham	30.1.18

MENTIONED IN DESPATCHES.

No.	Name.	Coy.	Date.
426	Sgt. A. Shurvell	D	1.1.16
1733	Sgt. A. Cook	B	,,
1744	Sgt. B. W. Fairman	A	4.1.17
*2488	Sgt. F. Newman	C	,,
200069	C.S.M. J. L. Garrett	C	25.5.17
200624	Sgt. C. H. Allsworth	A	,,
200728	L/C. Caiger, A.C. (attd. 145 Bde H.Q.)		,,
200026	R.Q.M.S. J. Burford	H.Q.	21.12.17
200187	Sgt. G. W. Grant	H.Q.	,,
200695	Sgt. L. S. Stratford (attd. 145 Bde H.Q.)		,,
200215	C.Q.M.S. H. J. Harmsworth	C	30.5.18
200176	Sgt. O. Frewin	H.Q.	,,
200485	Sgt. F. J. Clements	B	,,
200362	Sgt. H. J. Howse	A	,,
200075	Sgt. A. A. Alder	B	6.1.19
200274	Sgt. A. S. Garrett	H.Q.	,,

MENTIONED IN DESPATCHES—continued.

No.	Name.	Coy.	Date.
200662	Cpl. W. H. Goddard	H.Q.	6 1.19
203380	Cpl. L. D. Howells	H.Q.	,,
200696	L/C. R. Lewis	H.Q.	,,
200005	Cpl. C. E. Liebermann	H.Q.	3.6.19
200488	L/C. W. J. Jordan	H.Q.	,,
200626	C.Q.M.S. H. G. Haley	B	,,
200004	C.Q.M.S. W. A. Burgess	A	,,
200602	Sgt. G. Kimberley, M.M.	D	,,
200501	Sgt. W. T. Gray	C	,,
200457	Pte. C. F. J. Goodgame	A	,,

1/4th OXF. & BUCKS LT. INFTY. 85

OFFICIAL RECORD OF AWARDS.

(This Record includes only those awards made for Service with the Battalion).

BAR TO DISTINGUISHED SERVICE ORDER.

Lt.-Col. A. J. N. BARTLETT, D.S.O.
For conspicuous gallantry and devotion to duty during the Austrian attack of 15/6/18. By his skilful handling of his Battalion he maintained his position in spite of the line being penetrated on both flanks, thereby checking the enemy's advance, and enabling the line to be completely re-established by counter-attack. By his courage and coolness he set a splendid example to all ranks.

DISTINGUISHED SERVICE ORDER.

Major J. O. SUMMERHAYES [R.A.M.C.].
During all active operations in July and August 1916 he did exceptionally fine work as Medical Officer, always inspiring and cheering the men. On three occasions, after the Battalion had been relieved and he could leave his Regimental Aid Post, he went up to the front line trenches and organised the removal of wounded whom it had been impossible to move before. On the night of the 19/7/16 he spent the hours of darkness evacuating wounded from a front line trench S.W. of POZIERES, notwithstanding a barrage of gas shells, he himself also suffering from the gas.

Lt.-Col. A. J. N. BARTLETT.
For skill in command of his Battalion, which he led in many successful attacks. By his hard work and good organisation he maintained his Battalion in a high state of efficiency.

Major A. B. LLOYD BAKER [1st Bucks Battalion].
For continuous good work and devotion to duty as Second in Command of the Battalion. This officer has been previously recommended for his conspicuous good work in the field whilst with his own battalion.

WAR RECORD OF THE

Major P. PICKFORD, M.C.
For performing gallant and good work throughout the fight on 15/6/18. He was continually moving between the front line and Battalion Headquarters, and when the situation was critical he personally took a handful of men and placed them exactly where they were required. But for his splendid grasp of the situation and quick initiative the Battalion might several times have been surrounded.

BAR TO MILITARY CROSS.

Lieut. H. MILES, M.C.
On 14/5/18 he made a personal reconnaissance in daylight of the enemy's position at AVE. south of ASIAGO and noted a place obviously occupied by the enemy at night. He prepared a scheme for a fighting patrol consisting of his own platoon of 30 men, which he led with skill and daring during the same night, and attacked the enemy post. He led and directed the fight, which resulted in the capture of one prisoner, till he himself was severely wounded in the arm.

MILITARY CROSS.

Captain P. PICKFORD.
Whilst in PLOEGSTEERT WOOD on many occasions he was out in front of the line on reconnaissance work and working parties and by his example inspired the N.C.O.'s and men with confidence when new to their work. On 13/6/15 and 15/6/15 he crawled out by day about 400 yards to within 20 yards of the enemy trenches and discovered an old German sap which led into their trenches, and located the positions of their sentries.

Captain G. K. ROSE.
For useful work as Intelligence Officer, often going on patrol at night close to the German lines. His reports have always been good and his information accurate.

Major J. J. CONYBEARE.
For conspicuous bravery and coolness on 18/10/15 when his trench was heavily bombarded by enemy artillery and minenwerfer and was partially destroyed. He probably saved many lives by his coolness in directing the traffic personally in a very dangerous part of the trench, which was being bombarded by minenwerfer.

1/4th OXF. & BUCKS LT. INFTY. 87

*2/Lieut. F. E. JONES.
On the 23/6/16, though wounded in the leg, he led his platoon in a charge into the enemy's trenches, which they successfully captured before he would return to have his wound dressed.

The Rev. K. JACKSON [C.F.].
On the night 19/7/16 S.W. of POZIERES as Regimental Chaplain, when stretcher bearers were scarce, he voluntarily accompanied the Battalion Medical Officer and a relief party for evacuating wounded from a trench in the front line, whence it had not been possible to move them before the Battalion was relieved. He himself carried in a wounded man from the front line trench upwards of half-a-mile to a position of safety, through a barrage of gas shells.

*2/Lieut. C. E. R. SHERRINGTON.
On the night 13/8/16 he was in command of the left half of SKYLINE trench N.W. of POZIERES when the enemy made a strong counter-attack, both from his front and his left flank. He held on till almost surrounded and then withdrew his force in a most able manner, in the face of great odds maintaining his guard of the left flank the whole time and thus keeping the line intact.

Captain F. B. JONES.
For continuous good work in command of a company at all times and especially in the fighting around POZIERES. He led his men with complete disregard of personal safety and set a magnificent example to all ranks.

Captain E. E. BRIDGES.
For untiring work as Adjutant of his Battalion. During the fighting on the SOMME his energy and resource were invaluable, and he set an excellent example to all ranks.

*2/Lieut. R. H. WHITE [25th London Regiment.]
Accompanied by two men, he went out four times to examine the enemy wire, and, in spite of meeting several hostile parties, attained his objective and brought back very valuable information.

Captain G. H. GREENWELL.
On the night 16/3/17 while his force of two companies were assembling previous to a raid on LA MAISONETTE, they were suddenly caught in a hostile barrage. He kept his force well in hand till the hostile fire lessened, when he re-formed and carried out the original plan with complete success.

*2/Lieut. A. ALLAN.
In three separate attacks, at LA MAISONETTE on 17/3/17, at ROISEL on 26/1/17, and at RONSSOY on 5/4/17 his platoon was in the front wave. On each occasion, and especially at RONSSOY where he showed initiative in dealing with a strong point, he led his men with conspicuous ability and courage.

Lieut. T. R. FORTESCUE.
On the night 10/4/17 he led his company in the attack on GILLEMONT FARM with great courage and determination. Although three of phis latoon commanders and nearly half his force had become casualties, he re-organised his company and continued to advance to within 150 yards of the Farm in the face of heavy machine gun fire. As no further progress was possible owing to casualties he held on there until he could receive further orders, and finally he withdrew in good order when ordered to do so.

2/Lieut. H. MILES.
On 6/10/17 he was in command of a company, which was called upon at short notice to take over a portion of the front line, about the strength and position of which much doubt existed. He made a quiet personal reconnaissance, and afterwards led his company into the position which was then established beyond doubt, and also pushed the line 200—300 yards forward of where he found it.

Lieut. J. M. CONSTABLE.
At a critical moment on 15/6/18, when the enemy looked like breaking right through, he collected Battalion H.Q. details and led them out to fill a gap which successfully checked the enemy. During the whole day he was continually on the watch for the hostile attempts to get round our flank, and by his personal example of coolness and determination helped to keep the line intact.

2/Lieut. W. R. VINCE.
In the early morning of 15/6/18 after the enemy had penetrated our line he led forward his platoon of the reserve with great dash and drove back the enemy. After this he took up a position with his own men and others he collected which held good all day in spite of several hostile attacks.

Captain J. E. BOYLE.
For conspicuous gallantry and devotion to duty during a raid (on SEC 10/9/18). Under considerable enemy shelling he sited and taped out a forming-up line out of enemy observation, and

from this he ran forward tapes for each leading platoon. He then personally placed the party on the line and pointed out to platoon commanders their exact objectives. During the raid, despite enemy barrage, he laid out tapes towards the enemy's front line to guide the raiding party back, and he did not return to our lines until the whole party was in.

Captain W. H. ENOCH.
The fact that every platoon succeeded in reaching and mopping up its objective without a hitch (on 10/9/18) was mainly due to the untiring efforts of this officer. For the three days preceding the raid he worked unceasingly, with the result that no detail was overlooked. He accompanied the raiding party and by his personal example inspired all ranks.

2/Lieut. W. R. B. BROOKS.
During a raid on 10/9/18 this officer was the first to enter the enemy trench. He found a post at the point of entry and immediately charged it, capturing an officer and four men. He then organised his platoon so as to cover the left flank of the attack and remained in the enemy lines until the whole raiding party was out. He displayed fine dash and good leadership.

2/Lieut. J. F. WRIGHT.
Throughout the operation on 10/9/18 he displayed great courage and initiative. His platoon was told off for the task of attacking a portion of the enemy line from the rear, and by his cool and skilful leadership he accomplished a difficult manœuvre with complete success. He himself captured several prisoners and set a fine example to his men.

Captain J. E. MACKAY.
For continuous good work and gallantry in the line as Battalion Scout Officer. His untiring energy in training the Scouts when at rest and personal fine leadership in the line produced at all times most useful reconnaissance and absolutely reliable information.

2/Lieut. J. T. FOSTER.
For dash and energy as Battalion Scout Officer during the advance into AUSTRIA (November 1918) when he kept excellent touch with the situation by his scouts and carried out all reconnaissance and work of advance guard of the Battalion when it was isolated from the Brigade.

WAR RECORD OF THE

R.S.M H. E. BUCKINGHAM.
For conspicuous good work as Regimental Sergeant Major and initiative and coolness in action. His influence among the N.C.O.'s has been of immense benefit to the Battalion. His organising ability in improving the supply of ammunition in action has contributed largely to the success of operations. In an emergency during the Austrian attack in June 1918, he organised a party of Battalion H.Q. details, and successfully filled a gap thereby repelling an enemy attack.

Captain J. B. MATTHEWS [R.A.M.C.].
For conspicuous bravery and devotion to duty as Battalion Medical Officer. His personal example at all times in the line and especially during active operations at YPRES in 1917 and on the ASIAGO Plateau in June 1918, greatly inspirited the men. His organisation and handling of casualties in action was excellent and the high standard attained by the Battalion stretcher-bearers was due to his personal supervision.

2/Lieut. E. E. HOWELL.
For conspicuous good work and devotion to duty as a Platoon Commander. During the action of 15/6/18 his personal efforts helped to save a critical situation. During a raid on 10/9/18 in the neighbourhood of ASIAGO he set a fine example of leadership under very heavy shell-fire and during the advance into AUSTRIA in November 1915 he exhibited pluck and coolness.

ITALIAN SILVER MEDAL FOR VALOUR.

Captain J. E. MACKAY.
For fine leadership and personal gallantry as Battalion Scout Officer. When in the line south of ASIAGO he personally led all patrols on their first expedition to various points, which resulted in the capture of a prisoner, much useful information, and finally the total confinement of the enemy within his own lines.

Major P. PICKFORD, D.S.O., M.C.
As Battalion Commander he gave proof of great courage in carrying out an attack on 10/9/18 against strongly fortified enemy positions south of ASIAGO, an attack which had been accurately prepared by him. By his personal example he inspired his command to the brilliant attainment of all their allotted objectives.

1/4th OXF. & BUCKS LT. INFTY. 91

Captain W. P. POWELL.
He led his company in the attack on 10/9/18 and carried out the difficult operation of attacking the enemy front line from behind with complete success. Although burned by a smoke grenade which exploded prematurely, he continued to direct the attack and set a splendid example to all ranks.

ITALIAN BRONZE MEDAL FOR VALOUR.

2/Lieut. J. F. WRIGHT, M.C.
For courage and initiative in a raid on the enemy's trenches on 10/9/18.

ITALIAN CROCE DI GUERRA.

Lt.-Col. A. J. N. BARTLETT, D.S.O.
For tactical skill and good leadership in command of his Battalion in the successful advance into AUSTRIA (November 1918).

Captain W. H. ENOCH, M.C.
For untiring energy and capable organisation during the advance into AUSTRIA (November 1918).

2/Lieut. G. E. WEBSTER.
For most capable supervision and organisation of the Battalion Transport, especially during the advance into AUSTRIA, when he had personally to superintend the supply, by pack animals through most difficult country, of water, rations and stores which never failed.

DISTINGUISHED CONDUCT MEDAL.

*2207 Sergt. J. S. C. KING.
For good work since being in the country, in charge of working parties in PLŒGSTEERT WOOD. When about 120 yards from the German lines he did a lot of wiring, and was also of great assistance to the Intelligence Officer in observing the work done in the German lines.

2470 Pte. L. H. SENIOR.
On 18/10/15 during a heavy bombardment of one of the fire trenches, when he had gone to see the telephone wires, he showed great coolness and succeeded in re-opening communication directly the heavy bombardment ceased. He remained in charge of the station as one signaller was killed and the others were very much shaken. He has done consistent good work throughout the campaign.

1440 Sergt. H. A. CLARK.
In the attack on 23/7/16 he commanded the loading platoon of the assault, and when all the officers and Coy. Sergeant Major were casualties took charge of the remainder of the company, organised and led further attacks in the enemy's trenches, till he himself was wounded. His prompt action held back the enemy's counter-attacks till reinforcements arrived.

1362 Sergt. L. CROWE.
On the night 13/8/16 he was in charge of his platoon in SKYLINE TRENCH, N.W. of POZIERES, when the enemy made heavy counter attacks and gained a footing in that trench. He collected the remainder of his own and another platoon that were not casualties and made repeated bomb attacks down the trench. Though cut off from his Battalion he stuck to his ground and worried the enemy for 24 hours till relieved the following night, thereby preventing the enemy from consolidating the position.

2249 Cpl. E. A. MAZEY.
On 23/7/16 in the attack S.W. of POZIERES, when his own section was depleted, of his own initiative he organised a bomb section from another company and was successful in forcing back the enemy bombers, thereby securing the left flank, which was exposed. Again on the night 13/8/16, West of POZIERES, when the enemy had obtained a footing in our trench and a local counter-attack was in progress, he himself rushed alone along the parapet throwing bombs down amongst the enemy till he was wounded, losing an eye.

200100 C.S.M. W. J. COGGINS.
On the night 14/5/18 he was with a fighting patrol of one officer and 30 other ranks, which attacked an enemy post just outside the enemy wire South of ASIAGO. The officer became a casualty in the first rush, but C.S.M. Coggins immediately took charge and led the platoon after the retreating enemy, of whom one was taken prisoner and several killed. He set a splendid example of pluck and initiative in the attack and afterwards organised

1/4th OXF. & BUCKS LT. INFTY. 93

a rear-guard which prevented the enemy, now reinforced, from interfering with the carrying in of the wounded officer.

18430 Cpl. J. H. STRATFORD.
He showed conspicuous bravery and utter disregard of personal safety during the Austrian attack on 15/6/18. When attacked from behind he jumped on the parapet and single-handed killed six of the enemy with the bayonet. At one time he held a fire bay alone against a large body of the enemy. The splendid example he set till he was himself wounded was beyond all praise.

8672 L/Cpl. F. S. SPICER.
During the Austrian attack on 15/6/18 he organised and held a strong point with a section of men from different units. Although the line was several times penetrated on his flanks he maintained his position during the whole day thereby checking the hostile advance, at the same time capturing twelve prisoners.

200410 Cpl. F. R. CROMBLEHOLME.
During the raid on 10/9/18, when an enemy machine gun opened fire from the flank he immediately took his section and rushed the gun. After a hand-to-hand fight in which the officer attempted to bayonet him he succeeded in killing the officer and capturing the gun and the remainder of the team.

BAR TO MILITARY MEDAL.

201785 Sergt. W. N. HOBBS, M.M.
He displayed great initiative and dash during an attack at YPRES. When his Company was held up by heavy machine gun and rifle fire he organised and led a small party against an enemy strong point, but failed to take it, as the majority of his party were knocked out.

200229 Sergt. A. W. LEMMINGS, M.M.
After leading his men to the attack on 10/9/18 he showed good initiative in posting his Lewis gun on the flank and enabled another party to pass through to their objective. He then personally supervised the mopping up of his area, inspiring his men with the utmost confidence by his example of coolness.

13294 Pte. G. DANIELLS, M.M.
He showed striking personal courage during the raid on 10/9/18. He handled his Lewis gun with great skill and coolness and was largely instrumental in capturing a post of five men.

MILITARY MEDAL.

178 Sergt. L. H. GRIFFIN.
For consistent good work as Signalling Sergeant. On 18/10/15 when one of the fire trenches was heavily bombarded he was in the trench at the time and brought back the first information as to the state of affairs, having to crawl for some distance over the open to get back while the enemy were still bombarding.

2695 Sergt. J. H. MATTINSON.
He has many times undertaken useful patrol and reconnaissance work, particularly on 18/9/15, when he took out a patrol and acquired useful information of the ground and enemy's wire near the POINT. He has at all times shown great ability, energy, and devotion to duty.

1704 Sergt. B. W. FAIRMAN.
For consistent good work on patrol, having frequently brought back valuable information.

*2488 Sergt. F. NEWMAN.
For consistent good work on patrol, especially on 10/10/15, when he succeeded in bringing from the German wire the body of the man who had been killed on patrol.

2202 Sergt. J. WOOLNOUGH.
For great devotion to duty in controlling his section on the night of 4/5/16, when in charge of an isolated post, which was partially buried by minenwerfer fire and sniped by rifle grenades.

1671 Sergt. A. H. WOOTON.
For consistent coolness under fire and complete disregard of his own personal safety.

1579 L/Cpl. A. ADMANS.
For conspicuous gallantry on 18/10/16 in remaining in an advanced post throughout the day under extremely heavy shell fire, and taking charge of the post when the N.C.O. in charge had been disabled.

1938 L/Cpl. G. ASHPLANT.
For conspicuous devotion to duty while in charge of the company stretcher-bearers for over 14 months, especially on 7/5/16 when he rescued two seriously wounded men under heavy fire.

201089 L/Cpl. A. T. TURNER.
For consistent good work. His example and influence over the men have on many occasions proved invaluable.

1/4th OXF. & BUCKS LT. INFTY. 95

1427 Bandsman T. CARTER.
For consistent devotion to duty, showing great energy in attending to the wounded at all times and under all circumstances, frequently under heavy fire.

*1654 C.S.M. J. T. PEET.
For consistent good work as Platoon Sergeant. By his courage and cheerfulness on all occasions he has set the highest example to all.

*1776 Sergt. T. P. BARLOW.
For keeping his men to their work under fire on a wiring party, and for gallantry in attending to the wounded on the night of 9/4/16.

3637 (afterwards 201233) L/Cpl. T. WARD.
During the attack on the 23/7/16, he single-handed held back for 10 minutes a German party bombing up a trench while a fresh attack by us was being organised and more bombs fetched.

3530 Sergt. A. ENSTONE.
During the attack on 23/7/16 S.W. of POZIERES he did conspicuous good work with his platoon; though twice wounded he would not leave his post to be attended to till the position was consolidated.

*1700 Cpl. R. W. STEVENS.
On 16/8/16 West of POZIERES when in charge of an advanced post, although the remainder of the trench on either side was obliterated and the garrison withdrawn, he maintained his position and consolidated the post in a most able manner.

1585 L/Cpl. B. W. HARBOD.
After the attack S.W. of POZIERES during the morning 23/7/16 working as stretcher-bearer between the lines, he carried many wounded across the open into safety regardless of personal safety.

*2315 L/Cpl. T. W. HERMON.
On the night 13/8/16 he was in charge of a Lewis gun on the left flank of SKYLINE TRENCH N.W. of POZIERES. When attacked heavily from front and flank, he handled his gun in most able manner. When the party were almost completely surrounded he withdrew the gun, himself firing it all the while from the shoulder till they got back to a position suitable to cover the exposed flank, when he himself was wounded. His action kept the exposed flank secure and inflicted great loss on the enemy.

96   WAR RECORD OF THE

3057 Pte. L. W. HAWKINS.
During the night attack S.W. of POZIERES on 23/7/16 and during the morning following he constantly carried messages up to and from the front line across the open and under heavy shrapnel fire.

4262 Pte. A. MARGETTS.
After the attack S.W. of POZIERES on 19/7/16 acting as stretcher-bearer in an exposed piece of trench whence the wounded could not be moved, he remained voluntarily with them after the Battalion was relieved till they were safely evacuated the following night.

3616 Pte. F. G. MILLIN.
During the night attack S.W. of POZIERES on 23/7/16 and after daylight, when acting as runner from Battalion Headquarters he carried several messages across the open to the front line under very heavy fire.

*3584 Pte. E. W. THOMAS.
After the attack S.W. of POZIERES during the morning 23/7/16 working as a stretcher-bearer between the lines, he carried many wounded across the open into safety regardless of personal safety.

200335 Pte. T. H. SMITH.
For continuous gallantry on patrol when examining enemy wire in front of LA MAISONETTE and for obtaining most useful information about the same.

203615 Pte. J. E. GODWIN.
For continuous gallantry on patrol when examining enemy wire in front of LA MAISONETTE and for obtaining most useful information about the same.

200735 Sergt. W. H. MUDGE.
On 5/4/17 during the attack on RONSSOY he was in charge of the last platoon. When the attack showed signs of being held up by hostile machine gun fire he personally led his platoon forward, carrying forward the line that was held up, thus giving the required impetus for the final assault.

201049 L/Sergt. A. C. H. WIGGINS.
On 26/3/17 during the attack on ROISEL he led a patrol with skill and determination, facilitating a successful entry into the town. Afterwards he located and led an attack on an enemy machine gun which was holding up the attack of the company on his right flank, successfully dislodging it.

1/4th OXF. & BUCKS LT. INFTY. 97

200793 L/Cpl. B. BATTS.
On 5/4/17 during the attack on RONSSOY he displayed great initiative, coolness, and courage, and when he became detached from his platoon he led his section through the village, driving the enemy before him until he reached the final objective some 500 yards beyond.

201785 L/Cpl. W. N. HOBBS.
On 5/4/17 during the attack on RONSSOY he led his section with great dash and rallied them successfully after the outer fringe of the village had been taken. He afterwards succeeded in capturing or killing a party of over twelve of the enemy who were endeavouring to retire.

200899 L/Cpl. J. UPSTONE.
On 5/4/17 during the attack on RONSSOY he most successfully concentrated the fire of his Lewis gun on the main machine gun position of the enemy, finally silencing their fire and killing the entire team. His personal dash and daring use of his gun materially assisted the advance of his company.

200462 L/Cpl. F. G. WILSON.
On 5/4/17 during the attack on RONSSOY when the attack was checked by machine gun fire, he rallied his section round him, led them forward and captured the gun at the point of the bayonet.

200482 Pte. J. T. WHITE.
On 4/4/17 he was one of a patrol sent to obtain information about the enemy's position at RONSSOY. The N.C.O. and four others were casualties about 40 yards from a hostile machine gun in daylight. Pte. White took command at once, withdrew the remainder without further loss and afterwards led out a party to fetch in the wounded.

200631 Sergt. H. A. HARRIS.
In the attack on GILLEMONT FARM on 18/6/17, being in the left front platoon he took charge when his platoon commander was killed and also of the front platoon on his right which also had lost its commander. He established posts with what men remained, got in touch with his flanks and sent back word to his company commander.

200116 Cpl. R. J. COLLIER.
On 18/6/17 he and his section which belonged to the right flank platoon were told off to keep in touch with the platoon on his left. He lost communication with his own platoon but estab-

G

WAR RECORD OF THE

lished a post and as soon as it was dark joined up with his flanks, thus making the four platoons in touch.

200602 Cpl. G. KIMBERLEY.
In the attack on 18/6/17 he was directly responsible for turning the enemy out of rifle pits by the determined way he pushed on with his section. He was finally left with only two men of his section, but he rallied what was left of a Lewis gun section, established a post covering our left flank, and got in touch with the platoon on his right.

200774 L/Cpl. G. J. LEEDS.

201129 Pte. R. G. CHAMINGS.

203383 Pte. A. W. MAY.
After the attack on GILLEMONT FARM on 18/6/17 these stretcher-bearers moved about among the wounded under heavy shell and machine gun fire, thus reaching men who would otherwise have died of wounds. It was 2.30 a.m. before they brought the last stretcher case in, and it was entirely due to the good work they accomplished that nearly every man was accounted for.

201472 Pte. E. AYRES.
On 18/6/17 he did exceptionally well with his Lewis gun, accounting for several of the enemy and keeping down the enemy's rifle fire from the left of GILLEMONT FARM. The majority of the team had become casualties, but he continued to carry on irrespective of the enemy's heavy machine gun fire

200072 Sergt. F. HALEY.
On the night of 17/8/17 he did very good work in organising a party to get in the wounded. The shelling was very heavy at the time, but he persevered until all the wounded had been accounted for.

*200677 L/Cpl. C. C. GRAY.
He is specially mentioned for good work done not only in the attack on 16/8/17, but in previous engagements, when he has laid and repaired the telephone wires under very heavy fire.

201728 Pte. H. J. FINCH.
As a runner, he is specially recommended for the good work he did on 16/8/17 in carrying messages to Battalion Headquarters. Though buried by shells and sniped at by machine guns and rifles he carried on in a most courageous manner.

1/4th OXF. & BUCKS LT. INFTY. 99

200749 Pte. H. S. PEARCE.
For coolness and good work as stretcher-bearer in getting away wounded by day and night under continual rifle and machine gun fire, particularly in front of YPRES on 17/8/17.

200009 C.Q.M.S. W. J. LIEBERMANN.
As Company Q.M.S. he most efficiently got up food for his company during the Austrian attack on 15/6/18, afterwards organising a post on an exposed flank with cooks and men of different units which successfully held back the enemy for several hours.

202990 Sergt. A. DISBURY.
He showed great bravery and initiative when the front line was being heavily attacked on 15/6/18. He took up his platoon and formed a defensive flank, covering two platoons which would otherwise have been enveloped from the flank.

200209 Sergt. A. W. LEMMINGS.
On 15/6/18 he attacked two hostile machine guns with his men, and after killing the gunners, captured the guns and the remainder of the crews.

*203559 L/Sergt. G. T. WATERMAN.
He risked his own life during the bombardment on 15/6/18 in trying to find help for his wounded. He reconnoitred the front line just before the enemy attacked, bringing back useful information. He was then wounded and captured, but escaped again, and brought back valuable information concerning the enemy.

200790 L/Cpl. F. H. ATKINS.
He showed conspicuous gallantry and devotion to duty as stretcher-bearer, setting a splendid example of courage and cheerfulness during the attack on 15/6/18.

203418 L/Cpl. S. W. WILKS.
When in charge of a Lewis gun section in the front line on 15/6/18 he fought his gun till he was completely surrounded, his gun destroyed, and four of his men knocked out. He fought his way out through the enemy and continued to take part in the fight.

202164 L/Cpl. E. H. WYATT.
For conspicuous gallantry and determination in the use of his Lewis gun on the enemy when they were trying to get through our wire on 15/6/18. He afterwards formed a post with his gun on an exposed flank and checked and drove back a party of the

enemy which was trying to get round the flank with two machine guns.

266908 Pte. F. A. ALLEN.
He showed conspicuous bravery in the way he fought his Lewis gun on 15/6/18 even after he was wounded, killing large numbers of the enemy who were trying to work round the company's left flank.

13294 Pte. G. DANIELLS.
On 15/6/18 he assumed command of a section after the commander became a casualty and inspired the men to a great effort in holding up the enemy at a critical point. He afterwards led his section in a counter-attack and displayed remarkable courage, himself killing several of the enemy who refused to come out of a shelter.

9340 Pte. H. RICHARDS.
He showed the greatest bravery and determination during the Austrian attack on 15/6/18. After being turned out of the trenches he re-formed a small party and drove back the enemy at a critical moment, afterwards maintaining command and showing great initiative with his section.

29423 Pte. H. H. RYLAND.
For conspicuous gallantry and devotion to duty as runner, in carrying messages between reserve company headquarters and the front line during the very heavy bombardment of 15/6/18. He was wearing a gas mask all the time.

201858 Sergt. H. A. BURDEN.
He showed great courage and coolness and set a magnificent example to his men. Although excused duty he requested to be allowed to accompany the raiding party on 10/9/18.

201228 Sergt. A. G. COOPER.
As Platoon Sergeant he showed the utmost bravery during the raid on 10/9/18 and inspired his men with great keenness. He himself bombed several dug-outs and captured prisoners.

201552 Sergt. G. HARRIS.
As Platoon Sergeant on 10/9/18 he gallantly led his men to their objectives and was the first to enter the sunken road. His good leadership inspired all ranks with confidence and the success of this part of the operation was largely due to him.

200157 Sergt. T. F. WYNNE.
As Platoon Sergeant he showed courage and resource throughout

the raid on 10/9/18, moving his men up close to the barrage and himself leading the charge into the enemy trench.

200286 Cpl. W. G. CLEMENTS.
On 10/9/18 he displayed great courage in attacking an enemy machine gun which, with two of his Lewis gun team, he rushed, killing the gunner and capturing the gun and one prisoner.

203584 Cpl. E. T. OLLSON.
He led his section with great coolness and determination during the raid on 10/9/18, clearing dug-outs and killing or capturing many of the garrison of the trench. He set a fine example of bravery throughout.

201619 Cpl. E. RIXON.
During a raid South of ASIAGO on 10/9/18 he encountered a strong enemy post behind the front line. He led his section to attack them and himself bayonetted two of them and captured five.

200507 L/Cpl. J. T. DYER.
On 10/9/18 he led his section with great skill and determination, entering the enemy's trench at the exact point allotted to him and himself capturing three prisoners. With his section he then bombed a large dug-out from which seven prisoners were captured.

200519 L/Cpl. H. C. HARRIS.
On 10/9/18 when detailed to go forward from the enemy front line he handled his section with skill and courage, covering the advance of a platoon in rear and capturing five of the enemy.

26670 Bugler H. W. BENNETT.
He showed remarkable bravery and initiative in attacking the enemy's trench on 10/9/18. Several times he collected up scattered parties of men and led them himself, clearing the trench and capturing several prisoners.

10456 Pte. A. HALL.
He showed great dash and determination throughout the raid on SEC on 10/9/18. Calling upon a few men to follow him he rushed forward, attacked an enemy post and captured the entire garrison.

33015 Pte. F. PRICE.
On 10/9/18 he acted with dash as No. 1 of his Lewis gun team and handled his gun well. Immediately on crossing the enemy front line he pushed well forward and got into action on some retreating enemy. Later he gave covering fire on to a hostile machine gun and enabled another party to rush it.

WAR RECORD OF THE

200745 Pte. H. SAUNDERS.
On 10/9/18 he rushed an enemy machine gun, which was firing at another party, captured it and killed the crew.

265515 C.S.M. T. AVERY.
As Company Sergeant Major during the operations 1/11/18-3/11/18 he set a splendid example of energy and devotion to duty.

200274 Sergt. A. S. GARRETT.
During the advance into AUSTRIA, as Battalion Signal Sergeant, he showed great initiative and untiring energy in maintaining communication within the Battalion and with other units thereby greatly facilitating the rapid progress of operations.

203380 Sergt. L. D. HOWELLS.
As Battalion Scout Sergeant, during the operations North of ASIAGO 1/11/18-3/11/18 he organised and led several patrols, obtaining information of the utmost importance. As on other occasions he shewed initiative, dash, and fine leadership.

200362 Sergt. H. J. HOWSE.
On 1/11/18 North of ASIAGO this N.C.O. was acting C.S.M. of his company when it was ordered to fill in a gap between two attacking battalions. During a most difficult advance through thickly wooded country he set a splendid example of courage and determination, making a personal reconnaissance and leading his men up the most precipitous places to carry out his task.

200022 Cpl. G. T. DOUGLAS.
As N.C.O. in charge of the pack animals on 1/11/18 and 2/11/18 he showed untiring energy and determination in finding the Battalion and bringing up stores and rations to most inaccessible places, the most difficult part of the journey being carried out during darkness.

203908 L/Cpl. J. S. FARR.
During a daylight reconnaissance North of ASIAGO on 30/10/18 he set a splendid example of personal courage and fine leadership when his patrol came under heavy rifle and machine gun fire. It was due to his coolness and grasp of the situation that the patrol regained our lines without any casualties and brought in all the information required.

200602 L/Cpl. A. C. TOMLIN.
On several occasions he has shown great initiative and tactical

1/4th OXF. & BUCKS LT. INFTY.

skill in the handling of his Lewis gun section, setting a fine personal example himself.

11346 Pte. A. HUDSON.
For conspicuous bravery and devotion to duty as a runner. On many occasions he had most difficult tasks to carry out and has never failed.

MERITORIOUS SERVICE MEDAL.

200409 Sergt. H. F. JEYNES.
As Transport Sergeant during the whole time the Battalion has been on service from March 1915, he has shown untiring energy in keeping horses and personnel always up to a high state of efficiency.

200026 R.Q.M.S. J. BURFORD.
As Regimental Q.M.S. and previously as Company Q.M.S. he never spared himself in his efforts to ensure the efficient working of the supplies.

200251 C.Q.M.S. H. J. HARMSWORTH.
For consistent good work in the rank of Sergeant and Company Q.M.S. during the whole period the Battalion has been on active service.

200136 Sergt. A. G. E. RUSSELL.
For perpetual good work and devotion to duty in the capacity of Orderly Room Clerk during the whole period that the Battalion has been on active service since March 1915.

200009 C.Q.M.S. W. J. LIEBERMANN.
For constant good work and devotion to duty as Company Q.M.S. during the whole time the Battalion has been abroad. He set at all times a magnificent example of energy and cheerfulness.

200176 Sergt.O. FREWIN.
For conspicuous good work and devotion to duty as Battalion Pioneer Sergeant during the whole period the Battalion has been abroad.

200662 Cpl. W. H. GODDARD.
He has been Medical Officer's Orderly since the Battalion proceeded overseas in March 1915. He has shown gallantry and marked devotion to duty on every occasion when the Battalion has been in action.

ITALIAN SILVER MEDAL FOR VALOUR.

18430 Cpl. J. H. STRATFORD, D.C.M.
For conspicuous bravery and a magnificent example on the occasion of the Austrian attack on 15/6/18.

ITALIAN BRONZE MEDAL FOR VALOUR.

200410 Cpl. F. R. CROMBLEHOLME, D.C.M.
For capturing a machine gun and team on the occasion of a Battalion raid on 10/9/18.

CROCE DI GUERRA.

203397 Cpl. W. R. PRICE.
On 18/5/18 he had charge of a reconnoitring patrol looking for enemy patrols S.W. of ASIAGO. He thoroughly searched all the ground up to the enemy's wire till he located an enemy post. He himself shot the sentry, causing the enemy to stand to and open fire, thereby disclosing their position and strength.

201610 Cpl. E. RIXON, M.M.
For marked courage and good leadership on 10/9/18.

201233 (formerly 3637) Cpl. T. WARD, M.M.
On 10/9/18 he was in charge of a Lewis gun team sent forward to guard against counter-attack. He himself captured five of the enemy and set a splendid example to his men, pushing well forward and thereby preventing surprise, while the main raiding party was clearing dug-outs behind him. When the work was done he was the last of the raiding party to withdraw.

201259 L/Cpl. E. H. LUCKETT.
He was in charge of the Lewis gun section of his platoon, which he led to the attack on enemy dug-outs in a sunken road on 10/9/18. He was the first man to reach the objective, and set a magnificent example of courage and determination to his platoon.

203380 Sergt. L. D. HOWELLS, M.M.
For excellent reconnaissance and dash as Scout Sergeant.

BELGIAN CROIX DE GUERRE.

200262 L/Cpl. P. MILLIN.
For constant devotion to duty when in charge of stretcher-bearers during the attack on 23/7/16 and afterwards in trenches between 13/8/16 and 27/8/16, especially on this last occasion when he took his four men up to the newly captured trench and helped the wounded throughout the night under fire.

1/4th OXF. & BUCKS LT. INFTY.

OFFICERS PROCEEDING OVERSEAS
March 1915.

H.Q.

Lt.-Col. F. W. Schofield.
Major R. L. Ovey.
Capt. J. A. Ballard.
Major A. A. Bridgewater.
Capt. J. O. Summerhayes.
Lt. B. Long.
2/Lt. A. K. Gibson.

A.

Capt. R. R. S. Rowell.
Capt. J. J. Conybeare.
Lt. F. B. Jones.
2/Lt. C. R. Mason.
*2/Lt. C. J. S. Viner.

B.

†Capt. D. M. Rose.
*Capt. E. G. Dashwood.
†Lt. G. K. Rose.
†2/Lt. J. E. A. Cranmer.
2/Lt. H. A. Wilsdon.
*2/Lt. B. B. B. Brooks.

C.

Capt. E. C. Fortescue.
Capt. E. G. Coleman.
Lt. P. Pickford.
*Lt. I. E. Griffin.
††2/Lt. M. W. Edmunds.
2/Lt. C. C. Craig.

D.

*Capt. E. W. R. Hadden.
*Capt. J. N. Treble.
Lt. H. J. Deacon.
2/Lt. M. C. Cooper.
2/Lt. F. H. Grisewood.
*2/Lt. J. P. Hermon-Hodge.

† Wounded with Battalion.

OFFICERS BEFORE DEMOBILISATION
December 1918.

H.Q.

Lt.-Col. A. J. N. Bartlett, D.S.O.
Major P. Pickford, D.S.O., M.C.
†Capt. W. H. Enoch, M.C.
Capt. J. T. Corrie.
Capt. J. B. Matthews.
2/Lt. G. E. Webster.
Lt. J. M. Constable, M.C.
2/Lt. J. T. Foster, M.C.

A.

Capt. J. E. Boyle, M.C.
†Lt. H. F. Pearson.
Lt. F. W. H. Caudwell.
2/Lt. C. E. Moon.
2/Lt. W. R. B. Brooks, M.C.
2/Lt. G. M. Couche.

B.

†Capt. G. H. Greenwell, M.C.
Lt. H. S. Taylor.
Lt. H. A. Robertson.
Lt. A. L. Davis.
†Lt. D. S. L. Perkins.
2/Lt. W. R. Vince, M.C.

C.

††Capt. M. W. Edmunds.
Lt. W. P. Powell.
Lt. H. Barrett.
Lt. A. Roberts.
2/Lt. J. F. Wright, M.C.
2/Lt. H. Pickford.

D.

Capt. C. T. Davenport.
Lt. M. A. Oakford, M.C.
Lt. H. H. Dye.
†2/Lt. W. H. Carter.
2/Lt. L. T. Robinson.

† Wounded with Battalion.

1/4th OXF. & BUCKS LT. INFTY.

OFFICERS holding the Appointment of Commanding Officer, Second in Command, Adjutant, Company Commander, Quartermaster, Transport Officer, Intelligence Officer, and Medical Officer.

† Wounded with Battalion.

COMMANDING OFFICER.

4.8.14	Lt.-Col. A. Stockton.
1.1.15	Lt.-Col. F. W. Schofield.
25.4.15	Major R. L. Ovey.
11.5.15	*Lt.-Col. W. F. B. R. Dugmore, [D.S.O.
27.11.15	Lt.-Col. R. L. Ovey, D.S.O.
7.5.16	*Major E. W. R. Hadden.
4.6.16	Lt.-Col. A. J. N. Bartlett, [D.S.O.
6.5.17	Major P. Pickford, M.C.
6.6.17	†Lt.-Col. R. Stephens.
9.8.17	Lt.-Col. A. J. N. Bartlett, [D.S.O.

SECOND IN COMMAND.

1.1.15	Major R. L. Ovey.
20.9.15	Major J. A. Ballard.
6.11.15	Major R. R. S. Rowell.
16.1.16	Major J. J. Conybeare, M.C.
15.4.16	*Major E. W. R. Hadden.
10.6.16	*Major T. G. Grise.
13.6.16	Major E. C. Fortescue.
23.7.16	Major H. St. G. Schomberg.
27.4.17	Major P. Pickford, M.C.
7.7.17	Major P. A. Hall, M.C.
14.7.17	Major A. B. Lloyd-Baker, [D.S.O.
10.4.18	Major A. N. Waller, M.C.
17.4.18	Major G. R. Crouch.
16.5.18	Major P. Pickford, D.S.O. [M.C.

ADJUTANT.

4.8.14	Capt. J. A. Ballard.
20.9.15	Capt. F. H. Grisewood.
10.11.15	*Capt. I. E. Griffin.
11.2.16	†Capt. E. E. Bridges, M.C.
2.3.17	†Capt. W. H. Enoch.
4.8.17	Lt. J. C. B. Gamlen.
6.1.18	Lt. J. M. Constable, M.C.
7.4.18	†Capt. W. H. Enoch, M.C.

A COMPANY.

Capt. R. R. S. Rowell.
Capt. F. B. Jones.
Capt. J. D. Plowman.
†Lt. A. E. Crew.
Capt. J. E. Boyle, M.C.

B COMPANY.

†Capt. D. M. Rose.
*Capt. E. G. Dashwood.
Capt. J. J. Conybeare.
†Capt. G. K. Rose, M.C.
*Capt. B. B. B. Brooks.
†Capt. G. H. Greenwell, M.C.
*Capt. A. S. Wotherspoon.
†Capt. G. H. Greenwell, M.C.
Capt. H. S. Taylor.

OFFICERS HOLDING VARIOUS APPOINTMENTS—continued.

C COMPANY.

Capt. E. C. Fortescue.
Capt. E. G. Coleman.
Capt. P. Pickford, M.C.
††Capt. M. W. Edmunds.
†Capt. J. A. S. MacLean.
††*Lt. H. H. Jefferson.
*Capt. A. Allen, M.C.
Capt. W. P. Powell.
††Capt. M. W. Edmunds.

D COMPANY.

*Capt. E. W. R. Hadden.
*Capt. J. E. Blake.
*Capt. W. A. Wayman.
†Capt. J. H. Early.
Major R. R. S. Rowell.
Capt. T. R. Fortescue, M.C.
*Capt. R. P. Buxton.
†Capt. H. D. Hopcraft.
Capt. C. T. Davenport.

QUARTERMASTER.

4.8.14
to   Major A. A. Bridgewater.
15.11.17

Capt. J. T. Corrie.

TRANSPORT OFFICER.

Lt. A. K. Gibson.
*Capt. L. W. Birt.
Lt. G. E. Webster.

INTELLIGENCE OFFICER.

†Lt. G. K. Rose, M.C.
*Lt. J. S. C. King, D.C.M.
Lt. T. R. Fortescue.
†Lt. J. A. S. MacLean.
*Lt. R. H. White, M.C.
Lt. J. E. Mackay, M.C.
2/Lt. J. T. Foster, M.C.

MEDICAL OFFICER.

4.8.14
to   Major J. O. Summerhayes,
11.16.16   [D.S.O.
Lt. H. Fairfax.
Capt. T. Ferguson.
Lt. C. Baylor.
Capt. J. Ferguson.
Capt. J. B. Matthews.

1/4th OXF. & BUCKS LT. INFTY.

LIST OF OFFICERS
showing Period of Service with Battalion.

† Wounded with Battalion.
‡ Proceeded overseas with Battalion 29/3/15 in the Ranks.

Rank	Name.	Service with Battalion.	No of Months.
†2/Lt.	Affleck, R.	Sept./16-Jan./17	4
*Capt.	Allan, A. (M.C.)	Sept./16-June/18	21
Major	Ballard, J. A.	Aug./14-Nov./15	15
Lt.	Barrett, H.	Aug./17-Jan./19	17
Lt.-Col.	Bartlett, A. J. N. (D.S.O. and Bar)	June/16-June/17 Aug./17-Mar./19	31
Lt.	Baylor, C. [R.A.M.C.]	April/17	½
2/Lt.	Bennett, A.	Aug./17-Nov./17	2
2/Lt.	Benson, H. H.	July/17-Aug./17	1
*Capt.	Birt, L. W.	May/17-Sept./17	4
*Capt.	Blake, J. E.	Nov./15-July/16	8
2/Lt.	Bowler, W. J. B.	Nov./16-Dec./16	1
*2/Lt.	Bowman, C. H.	Mar./17-Aug./17	5
Capt.	Boyle, J. E. (M.C.)	Apr./17-Mar./19	23
†Capt.	Bridges, E. E. (M.C.)	Aug./15-May/17	18
Major	Bridgewater, A. A.	Aug./14-Nov./17	39
*Capt.	Brooks, B. B. B.	Aug./14-July/16	23
2/Lt.	Brooks, W. R. B. (M.C.)	Nov./17-Jan./19	14
*2/Lt.	Buttery, R. A.	Sept./17-June/18	9
*Capt.	Buxton, R. P.	Apr./17-June/18	14
†2/Lt.	Carter, A. W. [5th Middlesex.]	July/16-Aug./16	1
‡2/Lt.	Carter, W. H. [Bucks. Battalion]	Mar./18-Mar./19	12
2/Lt.	Caudwell, F. W. H.	Aug./17-Jan./19	17
†2/Lt.	Cochrane, D. E. [W. & C. Yeomanry.]	June/17-Aug./17	2
Capt.	Coleman, E. G.	Aug./14-Nov./15	15
Capt.	Constable, J. M. (M.C.)	Sept./17-Mar./19	18

WAR RECORD OF THE

OFFICERS PERIOD OF SERVICE—continued.

Rank	Name.	Service with Battalion.	No. of Months.
Major	Conybeare, J. J. (M.C.)	Aug./14-Apr./16	20
2/Lt.	Coombes, J. C. (M.C.)	Jan./16-Apr./16	3
Lt.	Cooper, M. C.	Jan./15-Jan./16	12
Capt.	Corrie, J. T.	Feb./18-Mar./19	13
	[6th Manchester.]		
.2/Lt.	Couche, G. M.	Oct./17-Nov./17	
		Dec./17-Jan./19.	13
Lt.	Craig, C. C.	Jan./15-Aug./16	19
†Lt.	Cranmer, J. E. A.	Sept./14/May/15	8
‡2/Lt.	Crew, A. E.	Apr./17-Aug./17	4
Capt.	Crouch, G. R.	Apr./18-May/18	1½
	[Bucks Battalion.]		
2/Lt.	Dadley, C. F.	Oct./16-Nov./16	1
2/Lt.	D'Arcy, G. W.	Sept./17-Aug./18	10
*Capt.	Dashwood, E. G.	Aug./14-May/15	9
Capt.	Davenport, C. T.	Oct./18-Mar./19	5
Lt.	Davis, A. L.	Sept./17-Nov./18	14
Capt.	Deacon, H. J.	Sept./14-Nov./15	15
*2/Lt.	Dinwoodie, D. W.	Sept./16-Apr./17	7
	[8th Scottish Rifles.]		
*Lt.	Doyne, P. D.	Aug./15-Sept./15	4
*Lt.-Col.	Dugmore, W. F. B. R.		
	[N. Staffs] (D.S.O.)	May/15-Dec./15	7
	[Killed in command of S. Staffs.]		
Lt.	Dye, H. H.	Oct./16-Dec./16	
		Nov./18-Mar./19	6
††‡Lt.	Early, J. H.	Nov./16-Aug./17	21
††Capt.	Edmunds, M. W.	Aug./14-July/16	
		Jan./17-Aug./17	34
		Nov./18-Mar./19	
2/Lt.	Ellis, J. E.	Nov./16	9 days
†Capt.	Enoch, W. H. (M.C.)	Jan./16-June/16	
		Nov./16-Aug./17	25
		Apr./18-Mar./19	
Lt.	Etty, J. L.	Oct./16-Nov./16	½
Lt.	Fairfax H. [R.A.M.C.]	Oct./16 Nov./16	1
*2/Lt.	Fawcett, E. H.	Oct./16-Nov./16	1
	[Killed with Bucks Battalion.]		
Capt.	Ferguson J. [R.A.M.C.]	Apr/17-June/17.	2
Capt.	Ferguson, T. [R.A.M.C.]	Nov./16-Mar./17	4

1/4th OXF. & BUCKS LT. INFTY. 113

OFFICERS PERIOD OF SERVICE—continued.

Rank.	Name.	Service with Battalion.	No. of Months
†2/Lt.	Fenwick, C. J. [5th Mid'sex.]	July/16	½
†2/Lt.	Fleeming, W. H.	Nov./16-Feb./17	3
Major	Fortescue, E. C.	Aug./14-Oct./15 Apr./16-July/16	17
Capt.	Fortescue, T.R. (M.C.)	June/16-July/16 Sept./16-Sept./17	25
2/Lt.	Foster, J. T. (M.C.)	Oct./17-Jan./19	15
Capt.	Fox, T. S. W.	Aug./14-Sept./14 Oct./17-Jan./18	4
*2/Lt.	Frieake, G. M.	Mar./16-July/16	5
Lt.	Gamlen, J.C.B. (M.C.)	Aug./16-Nov./16 Aug./17-Feb./18	9
*2/Lt.	Garlick, V.	Oct./16-June/18	20
2/Lt.	Gates, W. C.	Oct./17-Feb./18	4
2/Lt.	Gay, N.	Oct./17-Feb./18	4
Capt.	Gibson, A. K. (M.C.)	Sept./14-Feb./17	29
*2/Lt.	Gibson, H. E.	July/17-Aug./17	1
Capt.	Greenwell, G. H. (M.C.)	Oct./14-Mar./15 May/15-Nov./16 Jan./17-July/18 Oct./18-Jan./19	5 43
2/Lt.	Gribble, C. N. [Lanc. Hussars]	June/17-Nov./17	5
*Major	Grice, T. G. [2nd S.R.]	June/16	3 days
*Capt.	Griffin, I. E.	Aug./14-June/15 Nov./15-Feb./16	13
Lt.	Grisewood, F. H.	Sept./14-Nov./15	14
*Major	Hadden, E. W. R. [Died of appendicitis.]	Aug./14-June/16	22
*Lt.	Hall, T. N.	Jan./16-July/16	7
Major	Hall, P. A. (M.C.) [Bucks Battalion]	July/17	6 days
†The R.v	Henderson, J. H. [C.F.]	Mar./18-June/18 July/18-Sept./18	6
*2/Lt.	Hermon-Hodge, J. P.	Sept./14-May/15	8
2/Lt.	Hill, T. A.	Oct./16-Jan./17	2
†Capt.	Hopcraft, H. D.	Oct./17-Oct./18	12
2/Lt.	Howell, E. E. (M.C.)	Nov./17-Jan./19	14
*2/Lt.	Hughes, T. D.	Mar./16-May/16	2

H

114 WAR RECORD OF THE

OFFICERS PERIOD OF SERVICE—continued.

Rank.	Name.	Service with Battalion.	No. of Months.
2/Lt.	Hunt, A. N.	May/16-Aug./16	2
Lt.	Hunt, R. N. C.	Mar./16-Nov./16	8
*2/Lt.	Hunter, L. W.	Aug./16	6 days
*2/Lt.	Hutchins, D. M. [5th Middlesex]	July/16	1
The Rev.	Jackson, K.C. (M.C.) [C.F.]	May/16-Jan./17	8
††*2/Lt.	Jefferson, H. H.	June/16-Oct./16 Feb./17-Aug./17	10
Capt.	Jones. F. B. (M.C.)	Aug /14-Feb./17	30
†*2/Lt.	Jones, F. E. (M.C.)	Mar./16-July/16 Mar./17-Oct./17	11
2/Lt.	Judson, H. L.	Mar./15 July/15-June/16	10
2/Lt.	Kindell, A. O. W.	Nov./16	9 days
*2/Lt.	King, J. S. C. (D.C.M.)	Nov./15-May/16	6
†Lt.	King, J. V. [6th Middlesex]	July/16-Aug./16	2
†Lt.	Kirkwood, A. M. [7th S.R.]	Sept./16-Dec./16	3
*Lt.	Lake, R. St. G.	Mar./15 July/15-Nov./16	18
*Lt.	Lakin, C.	Mar./16-Aug./16	5
Lt.	Laurie, E.	Sept./17-Oct./18	11
††2/Lt.	Lay, F. C.	June/16-July/16 Nov./16-April/17	6
‡*2/Lt.	Lidsey, W. J. [Killed with R.F.C.]	June/16-Nov./16	5
2/Lt.	Lee, L. R. [R.W. Kents]	Sept./17-April/18	7
Major	Lloyd Baker, A. B. (D.S.O.)	July/17-April/18	9
Capt.	Long, B. (M.C.)	Aug./14-Jan./16	17
*2/Lt.	Luck, N. A. [R.W. Kents]	Sept./17-June/18	9
Capt.	Mackay, J. E. (M.C.)	May/17-May/18	12
†Capt.	MacLean, J. A. S.	Sept./16-Aug./17	11
2/Lt.	Maggs, E. G. [R.W. Kents]	Sept./17-Nov./17	2
2/Lt.	Mason, C. R.	Mar./15-Feb./16	11
Capt.	Matthews, J. B. (M.C.) [R.A.M.C.]	June/17-Dec./18	18

1/4th OXF. & BUCKS LT. INFTY. 115

OFFICERS PERIOD OF SERVICE—continued.

Rank.	Name.	Service with Battalion.	No. of Months.
2/Lt.	Meyrick, E. G. [5th Middlesex.]	July/17	10 days
†2/Lt.	Miles, H. (M.C. & Bar)	Sept./17-May/18	8
†2/Lt.	Millard, W. M. [Wounded with T.M.B.]	June/16-Feb./17	8
2/Lt.	Moon, C. E.	Oct./17-Mar./19	17
*2/Lt.	Moore, T.	Oct./17-June/18	8
2/Lt.	Morphy, P. A.	Sept./17	4 days
Lt.	Muriel, L. F.	Jan./19	½
†2/Lt.	Murphy, J. L.	Oct./17-June/18 July/18-Aug./18	9
2/Lt.	Northcote, H. J.	Oct./17	7 days
Lt.	Oakford, M. A. M. (M.C.) [M.G. C.]	Oct./18-Jan./19	3
2/Lt.	Ovenstone, J. J.	Oct./17	7 days
Lt.-Col.	Ovey, R. L. (D.S.O.)	Aug./14-May/16	20
†2/Lt.	Paxton, H. R. [8th S.R.]	Sept./16-Dec./16	3
†2/Lt.	Pearson, G. E.	June/16-Aug./16 Feb./17-May/17	5
†Lt.	Pearson, H. F.	June/16-Mar./17 Sept./18-Mar./19	16
‡Lt.	Perkins, D. S. L.	Sept./17-June/18 Aug./18-Mar./19	16
2/Lt.	Pickford, H.	Dec./18-Mar./19	3
Major	Pickford, P. (D.S.O., M.C.)	Aug./14-Jan./17 April/17-June/17 May/18-Sept./18 Dec./18-Mar./19	40
2/Lt.	Pitts, G. A.	Mar./17-May/17	2
Capt.	Plowman, J. D. [5th Middlesex]	July/16-Aug./17	13
*2/Lt.	Powell, C. H. [Killed with R.F.C.]	Mar./16-April/16 Sept./16-Dec./16	4
Lt.	Powell, W. P. [Bucks Battalion]	Dec./16-Mar./19	27
Lt.	Proctor, A. W.	Mar./17-June/17	3
2/Lt.	Pullman, H. J. [Bucks Battalion]	Nov. /16	1
2/Lt.	Ramsey, R. G. [7th S.R.]	Sept./16-Nov./16	2

116 WAR RECORD OF THE

OFFICERS PERIOD OF SERVICE—continued.

Rank	Name.	Service with Battalion.	No. of Months.
*2/Lt.	Rawlinson, G. M.	Mar./16-July/16	4
Lt.	Richardson, M. C.	July/15-Jan./16	6
Lt.	Roberts, A.	Oct./17-Mar./18	
		Oct./18-Jan./19	8
Lt.	Robertson, H. A.	Nov./18-Mar./19	4
‡2/Lt.	Robinson, L. T.	Nov./18-Jan./19	2
†Capt.	Rose, D. M.	Aug./14-May/15	9
†Capt.	Rose, G.K. (M.C. and Bar)	Aug./14-April/16	20
Major	Rowell, R. R. S.	. Aug./14-Dec./15	
		Nov./16-June/17	23
2/Lt.	Saddington, W. H.	Aug./16-Nov./16	2
	[5th Middlesex]		
*2/Lt.	Salmon, A. F.	July/17-Aug./17	1
Lt.-Col.	Schofield, F. W. (C.M.G.)	Aug./14-April/15	9
Major	Schomberg, H. St. G. (D.S.O.)	July/16-April/17	9
	[1st East Surrey]		
†'Lt.	Scott, W. D.	Oct./16-Nov./16	
	[Killed with 2/4th Battalion]	July/17-Aug./17	2
2/Lt.	Shepherd, J. G.	June/16	½
2/Lt.	Sherrington, C. E. R. (M.C.)	June/16-Oct./16	4
†Lt.	Smith, E. E.	Mar./16-July/16	4
2/Lt.	Smith, G. G.	Jan./17-April/17	3
†2/Lt.	Smith, S.	April/16-July/16	3
2/Lt.	Spaven, L. C.	Sept./17-Nov./17	2
2/Lt.	Stafford, C. S.	Oct./17	7 days
2/Lt.	Stenner, R. S.	Oct./17	7 days
†Lt.-Col.	Stephens, R.	June/17-Aug./17	2
The Rev.	Streatfeild, F. (C.F.)	July/15-Mar./16	8
Major	Summerhayes, J. O. (D.S.O.)	Aug./14-Oct./16	26
	[R.A.M.C.]		
†‡2/Lt.	Swatridge, J.	July/17-Aug./17	1
Capt.	Taylor, H. S.	June/16-July/16	
		Nov./17-Mar./19	17
2/Lt.	Tetley, W. S.	Mar./17-Oct./17	7
†2/Lt.	Thompson, A. C.	July/16-Aug./16	2
	[5th Middlesex]		
2/Lt.	Townsend, F. O.	June/16	
		Jan./17	
		May/17-June/17	3
*Capt.	Treble, J. N.	Aug./14-Oct./15	14

1/4th OXF. & BUCKS LT. INFTY.

OFFICERS PERIOD OF SERVICE—continued.

Rank	Name.	Service with Battalion.	No. of Months.
*2/Lt.	Twelvetrees, B.	Sept./17	7 days
	[Killed with 1/5th Glouc. Regt.]		
Lt.	Vince, W. R. (M.C.)	Sept./17-Mar./18	18
*2/Lt.	Vokes, B.	Jan./17-Feb./17	1
*Lt.	Vyner, C. J. S.	Aug./14-July/15	12
2/Lt.	Wallace, W. J. L.	May/17-July/17	2
Major	Waller, A. N. (M.C.)	April/18	½
	[5th Glouc. Regt.]		
*Capt.	Wayman, W. A.	Sept./14-Mar./15	
		Jan./16-Aug./16	13
Lt.	Webster, G. E.	Oct./17-Mar./19	17
*2/Lt.	White, R. H. (M.C.)	Aug./16-Aug./17	11
	[25th London Regt.]		
†*2/Lt.	Wilkins, V. S.	Mar./17-April/17	
	[Died of influenza.]	Aug./17-Jan./18	5
Lt.	Wilsdon, H. A.	Sept./14-Jan./16	16
†2/Lt.	Wincer, E. C. H.	Mar./17-Aug./17	5
*Capt.	Wotherspoon, A. S.	Sept./16-Aug./17	11
	[8th S. R.]		
2/Lt.	Wright, J. F. (M.C.)	Oct./17-Jan./19	15
Lt.	Wrong, H. H.	Jan./16-Nov./16	10

ROLL OF WARRANT OFFICERS AND SPECIAL DUTY SERGEANTS OVERSEAS.

† Mentioned in Despatches.
c Subsequently obtained a Commission.

R.S.M.

*Adams, A. S.
*Lane, W. R.   30.5.15
*Pearce, E. J.   26.7.15
*Lane, W. R.   12.2.16
Buckingham, E. (M.C.) 11.9.17

R.Q.M.S.

Eagle, W. R.
Burford, J.   4.1.17
Liebermann, W. J.   23.1.17
†Burford, J. (M.S.M.)   9.4.17

A COY. S.M.

Nutt, D.
*Fincher, E. F.
cHeritage, H. J.
Saxton, C. L.
cFairman, B. W.
Lane, P. T.
cAllsworth, C. H.
Coleman, J.
cCoggins, W. J. (D.C.M.)
Lord, A. H.
Favell, C.

B COY. S.M.

Bishop, T. C.
Wicks, J. D.
cGodfrey, F. C.
cDuke, W. D.
Avery, T. (M.M.)

C COY. S.M.

cButler, H. A.
Giles, B. J.
†cGarrett, J. L.
cCoggins, W. J. (D.C.M.)
Coleman, J.

D COY. S.M.

cHill, J.
Lane, W. R.
Bunting, R.
*Peet, J. T. (M.M.)
cMcCulloch, J.
Wooton, A. H. (M.M.)
Green, J. V.
Harris, H. A.
Kimberley, G. (M.M.)
Woodcock, W. (M.M.)

WAR RECORD OF THE

ROLL OF WARRANT OFFICERS, &c.—continued.

A COY. Q.M.S.

*Fincher, E. F.
†Burgess, W. A.

B COY. Q.M.S.

Lane, W. R.
Bowen, C. E.
Burford, J.
†Haley, H. G.

C COY. Q.M.S.

Giles, B. J.
cPlummer, W. E. D.
†Harmsworth, H. J. (M.S.M.)

D COY. Q.M.S.

Ranson, A.
Shurvell, A.
Liebermann, W. J.
Green, J. V.
Liebermann, W. J. (M.M., M.S.M.)

SGT. BUGLER.

Liebermann, W. J.
Biggs, J. T.
Colborne, R. G.

ORDERLY ROOM SGT.

Overton, W. H.
Russell, A. G. E. (M.S.M.)

SIGNAL SGT.

Griffin, L. H. (M.M.)
†Garrett, A. S. (M.M.)

SCOUT SGT.

*cKing, J. S. C., (D.C M.)
†Grant, G. W.
†Howells, L.D. (M.M.)

TRANSPORT SGT.

Jeynes, H. F. (M.S.M.)

PIONEER SGT.

Parsons, W.
†Frewin, O. (M.S.M.)

SGT. MASTER COOK.

Cox, W.
Moss, B. F.
†Alder, A. A.
Baker, F. W.

SGT. SHOEMAKER

Knapp, W.

PROVOST SGT.

Earl, F.
Collett, J. C.

MESS SGT.

Bensley, J. L.

BAND SGT.

Liebermann, F.
Liebermann, C. E.

ARM. STAFF SGT.

Carver, W. J.

1/4th OXF. & BUCKS LT. INFTY. 121

ROLL OF SERGEANTS OVERSEAS.

† Mentioned in Despatches.
c Subsequently obtained a Commission.
d Proceeded overseas as Sergeant.

A COMPANY.

dBurgess, W. A.
dAllsopp, H. C.
dFoster, C.
dWarrell, J. E.
cdHeritage, H. J.
dChapman, P. W.
dSaxton, C. L.
*cdRobinson, W.
dWyatt, W. C.
Gilliver, H.
Cox, G. J.
Hinton, W.
Evans, G. H.
†cFairman, B. W. (M.M.)
*Price, O.
*Smith, N.
cMullis, E. V.
cEnstone, A. (M.M.)
cRamsay, W. A.
Coleman, G. E.
†cAllsworth, C. H.
Lane, P. T.
*Burden, G. H.
cMiller, R. P.
Hunt, R.
†Howse, H. J. (M.M.)
Dudley, W.
Butcher, J. R.
Wheeler, E. J.
Patient, S. H.
Hearne, E. H.
Gibbs, W. A.
Upstone, J. (M.M.)
Hollis, J. H.
Liebermann, C.
Burden, H. A. (M.M.)

Lord, A. H.
Simpson, A.
*Harris, W. C.
Gurr, R.
Fisher, H. C.

LANCE-SERGEANTS.

Gray, F. A.
Phillips, F. J.
*Wright, J. R.
Willis, H. J.
Lane, W. H.
Carder, A.
Lewing, S.

B COMPANY.

dLane, W. R.
dBowen, C. E.
dBurford, J.
dBrooks, A.
dWilliams, E. J.
dAndrews, P. C.
dCooper, L. F.
*dWilks, M. B.
cdEarly, J. H.
dWarne, A. V.
cdSmith, S.
*cKing, J. S. C.
Drewitt, C. E.
Jarvis, A. F.
cRobinson, L. T.
†*Cook, A.
*Barnes, W.
Miles, E. J.
cDuke, W. D.
Bevill, R. W.

WAR RECORD OF THE

ROLL OF SERGEANTS OVERSEAS—continued.

cRabett, C. J. W.
Andrews, P.C.
Wicks. J. D.
Jeacock. H. W.
Cook, H.
cAbraham, J. H. (M.M.)
Mumford, W.
Baston, H. C.
†Clements, F. J.
Mudge, W. H. (M.M.)
*Grimsley, J. H.
Admans, A. (M.M.)
Wiggins, A. C. H. (M.M.)
Whareham, F. G.
Cooper, A. G. (M.M.)
Miller, G.
*cMiles, S. J.
Haley, F. (M.M.)
Eeley, W. H.
cHobbs. W. N. (M.M. and Bar)
Lewis, R. G.
cSpiller, R. C.
Lemmings, A. W. (M.M. and Bar)
Sallis, P. W.
Collett, F. A.
Clarke, G. R.
cMayer, A. H.
Dunkeley, G. W.
Woodward, P. C.

LANCE-SERGEANTS.

*cStevens, R. W. (M.M.)
*Norwood, A.
Harris, G. (M.M.)
*Waterman, G. T. (M.M.)

C COMPANY.

cdPlummer, W. E. D.
dButler, G.
*dBoneham, W.
dBeck, K.
dStone, R. A.
dCanning, A. O.

cdGarrett, J. L.
dHarmsworth, J.
Catch, F.
Mattinson, J. H. (M.M.)
*Brooks, P.
Underwood, J.
Crowe. L. (D.C.M.)
cHarvey, A. E.
†*Newman, F. (M.M.)
Woolnough, J. (M.M.)
Wallin, W.
Collett, J. C.
Taylor, G. A.
Field, D. W.
cGodfrey, F. C.
*Drewitt. A.
Peddar, P.
cMoase, F. S. B.
*Singleton, A. J.
Newton, C. E.
cCoggins, W. J.
Paintin, G.
Edwards, F.
Walton. H.
Head, F. J.
Wynne, T. F. (M.M.)
Palmer, W.
Wright, H. J.
cAdams, C.
Earis, G.
†Gray, W. T.
Bandy, F. G.
Harrall, T.
Floyd, G.
*Isham, F. L.
Willoughby, L. E.

LANCE-SERGEANTS.

Prescott, H. E.
Holiday, T.
Morse, R. W.
*Butt. H.
*Sargood, R.
Disbury, A. (M.M.)

1/4th OXF & BUCKS LT. INFTY.

ROLL OF SERGEANTS OVERSEAS—continued.

D COMPANY.

dBunting, R. S.
†dShurvell, A.
dLiebermann, W. J.
dYoung, J.
dTownsend, H.
dBlackham, G.
*dPeet, J. T.
dDix, H.
dClarke, H. A. (D.C.M.)
cMcCullock, J.
Bennett, H. W.
*Barlow, T. P. (M.M.)
Page, J.
Pugh, C. R. J.
Bunting, R.
*Herbert, J. H.
Wooton, A. H. (M.M.)
Dunkley, W. G.
*Herbert, W. G.
Miller, A. H.
*Cook, F.
Green, J. V.
Burford, G.
Hardy, C.
Harris, H. A. (M.M.)
Grant, G. W.
Binder, F. C.

Taylor, C. H.
*Ross, A.
Castle, A.
*French, A.
Bird, W. J.
Holmes, E. W.
†Kimberley, G. (M.M.)
Coleman, J.
Crook, A. J.
Harbod, B. W. (M.M.)
Best, A. R.
Eustace, A.
Higgs, F. C.
Cook, A. G.
Green, F.
Williams, A. W.
Dudley, B.

LANCE-SERGEANTS.

Brice, J.
Jemmett, G.
cHurst, E. F.
Rutter, F. J.
Harris, R.
Collier, R. J. (M.M.)
Dudley, W. E.
Shaw, R.
Carter, F. P.

1/4th OXF. & BUCKS LT. INFTY.

ROLL OF N.C.O.s and MEN who served with the Battalion throughout the Campaign.

† Mentioned in Despatches.
a Pre-War Territorial.
b Territorial Efficiency Medal.

WARRANT OFFICERS.

†abR.Q.M.S. Burford, J. (M.S.M.)	H.Q.
†C.Q.M.S. Haley, H. G.	B
†aC.Q.M.S. Harmsworth, H. J. (M.S.M.)	C
S./Sgt. Carver, W. S. [A.O.C.]	H.Q.
abSgt. Bugler Colborn, R. G.	H.Q.

SERGEANTS.

Cook, A. G.	D
Crook, A. J.	D
†aFrewin, O. (M.S.M.)	Pioneer
†aGarrett, A. S. (M.M.)	Signals
†Gray, W. T.	C
Green, F.	D
Jeynes, W. (M.S.M.)	Transport
†Kimberley, G. (M.M.)	D
aRussell, A. G. E. (M S.M.)	Ord. Room
Sallis, P. W.	A

CORPORALS.

abBiggs, J. T.	Q.M. Stores
abDouglas, G.	Transport
Florey, W. H.	A
†Goddard, W. H. (M.S.M.)	Medical
†Jordan, W. J.	Transport
Launchbury, C.	Signals
†abLiebermann, W. L.	Medical
abSimms, W. E.	D

LANCE-CORPORALS.

aAnslow, F. C.	B Cook
Atkins, F. H. (M.M.)	D Stretcher-Bearer
Brannan, M. A.	Postman
aCallow, A. H.	C Storeman
abColes, L. J.	Signals
Cope, E.	Tailor
abDunn, T.	Transport
Dyer, J.	A
Goddard, H. R.	Q.M. Stores
aKing, W. C.	Q.M. Stores
abPayne, W. H.	Bugler
Purnell, E. A.	Police
Rooke, A. J.	A Storeman
aTaylor, W. E.	C Cook
Teague, H. R.	Bugler
Trafford, C. W.	D Cook
Turner, L. H.	Transport
Willcocks, C. H.	B Signals

N.C.O.s AND MEN WHO SERVED THROUGHOUT, &c.—continued.

PRIVATES.

aAdams, C. H.	Transport
Amos, A. J.	C
aArnold, W. G.	Transport
aAshton, J.	C
Baxter, W.	H.Q. Servant
Bettridge, H.	Transport
Betts, J. J.	Transport
Blackwell, J. H.	Barber
aBrooks, J.	A
Brown, G.	Barber
Buckle, P	A
aBurton, F.	H.Q. Cook
abClewer, F.	Pioneer
aCompton, L. J.	C Mess
abEarl, A.	Tailor
Edwards, R. W.	Transport
Franklin, W. H.	Tailor
Franklin, C. J.	D Cook
aGardner, H.	Transport
aGardner, P.	H.Q. Orderly
abGardner, W. C.	C
aGibbs, C. E.	Transport
aGrimstone, E. F.	C Signals
aHands, L. F.	C
aHoare, E. A.	Tailor
aHolton, J.	Transport
aHunneyball, T. W.	Signals
aInwood, E. J.	H.Q. Orderly
Jackson, G. M.	C
aKing, T. C.	Signals
aKing, J.	H.Q. Orderly
Kinvig, P. J.	Signals
Mace, H. R.	Transport
Mold, T. R.	Transport
Newbold, G. A.	C
Parrott, J. G.	Transport
Pavitt, H. J.	Pioneer
aPengilley, B. I.	D Servant
Ross, J. J.	B Servant
Slaymaker, H.	Transport
Skinner, E. H.	Signals
aSkuce, W.	Signals
Smith, E. J.	Transport
aTemple, J. H.	Transport
aWhite, H.	Signals
White, J. T. (M.M.)	C
Wilks, A.	H.Q. Orderly

1/4th OXF. & BUCKS LT. INFTY. 127

N.C.O.s and Men not on preceding List entitled to Territorial Efficiency Medal still serving with Battalion before Demoblisation.

WARRANT OFFICERS.

†C.Q.M.S. Burgess, W. A.	A
C.Q.M.S. Liebermann, W. J. (M.M., M.S.M.)	D

SERGEANTS.

Alder, A.A.	H.Q,
Disbury, A. (M.M.) [From Bucks Battalion.]	C
Eeley, W.	B
Knapp, W.	H.Q.
Lewis, R. G.	B
Liebermann, C. E.	H.Q.

LANCE-CORPORALS.

Battley, W. [From Q.O.O.H.]	C
Clements, W. G.	A
Roche, T. B. [From Bucks Battalion.]	H.Q.

PRIVATES.

Moss, J.	H.Q.
Saxton, H.	B

www.ingramcontent.com/pod-product-compliance
Lightning Source LLC
Chambersburg PA
CBHW071006160426
43193CB00012B/1933